REVISE EDEXCEL GCSE (9–1)
Religious Studies B
CATHOLIC CHRISTIANITY AND ISLAM
REVISION WORKBOOK

Series Consultant: Harry Smith

Author: Tanya Hill

Also available to support your revision:

Revise GCSE Study Skills Guide   9781447967071

The **Revise GCSE Study Skills Guide** is full of tried-and-trusted hints and tips for how to learn more effectively. It gives you techniques to help you achieve your best – throughout your GCSE studies and beyond!

Revise GCSE Revision Planner   9781447967828

The **Revise GCSE Revision Planner** helps you to plan and organise your time, step-by-step, throughout your GCSE revision. Use this book and wall chart to mastermind your revision.

For the full range of Pearson revision titles across KS2, KS3, GCSE, Functional Skills, AS/A Level and BTEC visit:
www.pearsonschools.co.uk/revise

Contents

Catholic Christianity

1 Catholic beliefs
1. The Trinity
2. God as a Trinity of persons
3. Creation
4. The significance of the Creation account
5. The Incarnation
6. Events of the Paschal Mystery
7. Jesus' life, death and resurrection
8. Eschatology

2 Marriage and the family
9. Marriage
10. Sexual relationships
11. Families
12. Support for the family in the Catholic parish
13. Family planning
14. Divorce
15. Men and women in the family
16. Gender prejudice and discrimination

3 Living the Catholic life
17. Sacramental nature of reality
18. Liturgical worship
19. Liturgy of the funeral rite
20. Prayer
21. Popular piety
22. Pilgrimage
23. Catholic social teaching
24. Mission and evangelism

4 Matters of life and death
25. Origins of the universe
26. Sanctity of life
27. Origins of human life
28. Abortion
29. Life after death
30. Non-religious arguments against life after death
31. Euthanasia
32. Issues in the natural world

5 Crime and punishment
33. Justice
34. Crime
35. Good, evil and suffering
36. Punishment
37. Aims of punishment
38. Forgiveness
39. Treatment of criminals
40. Capital punishment

6 Peace and conflict
41. Peace
42. Peacemaking
43. Conflict
44. Pacifism
45. The Just War theory
46. Holy war
47. Weapons of mass destruction
48. Issues surrounding conflict

7 Philosophy of religion
49. Revelation
50. Visions (1)
51. Visions (2)
52. Miracles
53. Religious experiences
54. The design argument
55. The cosmological argument
56. The existence of suffering
57. Solutions to the problem of suffering

8 Equality
58. Human rights
59. Equality
60. Religious freedom
61. Religious prejudice and discrimination
62. Racial harmony
63. Racial discrimination
64. Social justice
65. Wealth and poverty

Islam

1 Muslim beliefs
66. The Six Beliefs of Islam
67. The five roots of 'Usul ad-Din in Shi'a Islam
68. The nature of Allah
69. Risalah
70. Muslim holy books
71. Malaikah
72. Al-Qadr
73. Akhirah

2 Marriage and the family
74. Marriage
75. Sexual relationships
76. Families
77. The family in the ummah
78. Contraception
79. Divorce
80. Men and women in the family
81. Gender prejudice and discrimination

3 Living the Muslim life
82. The Ten Obligatory Acts of Shi'a Islam
83. The Shahadah
84. Salah
85. Sawm
86. Zakah and khums
87. Hajj
88. Jihad
89. Celebrations and commemorations

4 Matters of life and death
90. Origins of the universe
91. Sanctity of life
92. The origins of human life
93. Muslim attitudes to abortion
94. Death and the afterlife (1)
95. Death and the afterlife (2)
96. Euthanasia
97. Issues in the natural world

5 Crime and punishment
98. Justice
99. Crime
100. Good, evil and suffering
101. Punishment
102. Aims of punishment
103. Forgiveness
104. Treatment of criminals
105. The death penalty

6 Peace and conflict
106. Peace
107. Peacemaking
108. Conflict
109. Pacifism
110. The Just War theory
111. Holy war
112. Weapons of mass destruction
113. Issues surrounding conflict

7 Philosophy of religion
114. Revelation
115. Visions
116. Miracles
117. Religious experiences
118. The design argument
119. The cosmological argument
120. The existence of suffering
121. Solutions to the problem of suffering

8 Equality
122. Human rights
123. Equality
124. Religious freedom
125. Prejudice and discrimination
126. Racial harmony
127. Racial discrimination
128. Social justice
129. Wealth and poverty

Exam skills
130. (a) type questions
131. (b) type questions
132. (c) type questions
133. (d) type questions

134. Answers

• •

A small bit of small print
Edexcel publishes Sample Assessment Material and the Specification on its website. This is the official content and this book should be used in conjunction with it. The questions in this Workbook have been written to help you practise every topic in the book. Remember: the real exam questions may not look like this.

Had a go ☐   Nearly there ☐   Nailed it! ☐

Catholic Christianity — Catholic beliefs — Papers 1, 2 and 3

The Trinity

Guided 1 Outline **three** ways the Trinity is reflected in worship for Catholics today.

> Complete this answer by giving two further ways in which the Trinity is part of Catholic worship. Write each answer in a separate sentence.

The Trinity is part of Catholic baptism services when the sign of the cross is made. ....

....

....

....

....

....

(3 marks)

Guided 2 Explain **two** reasons why the role of the Father in the Trinity is important to Catholics.

In your answer you must refer to a source of wisdom and authority.

The role of the Father shows God as the powerful creator of the world. ....

....

....

....

> Each of these reasons needs developing. To do this, add another sentence or two that expands on the idea given – you could add an example or more information about the point made. Then, link one of your reasons to a quote from a source of authority – for example, the Nicene Creed or the Bible.

....

....

It shows God the Father sending his son Jesus to the world in human form.

....

....

....

....

....

(5 marks)

God as a Trinity of persons

In this question, 3 of the marks awarded will be for your spelling, punctuation and grammar, and your use of specialist terminology.

1 "Belief in the Trinity is the most important belief for Catholics."

Evaluate this statement considering arguments for and against.

In your response you should:

- refer to Catholic teachings
- reach a justified conclusion.

> Begin your answer by considering reasons why Catholics may **agree** with this statement – for example, the importance of the Trinity as a part of the Nicene Creed, or what the Trinity tells Catholics about the nature of God.

....
....
....
....
....
....
....

> The next part of your answer needs to consider reasons why some Catholics (as well as other Christians) may **disagree** with the statement. Consider other important teachings such as helping others or redemption. Remember that this part of your answer may require you to apply knowledge from other parts of the specification. You need to include several reasons.

....
....
....
....
....
....

> Having considered all the reasons, you need to offer a justified conclusion to your answer. This means acknowledging other views, but stating the reasons why you feel that your conclusion is correct.
>
> Remember, there are 3 marks available for spelling, punctuation and grammar (SPaG), so check through your answer carefully.

....
....
....
....

(15 marks)

Please complete your answer on your own paper if you need more space.

Had a go ☐   Nearly there ☐   Nailed it! ☐

Catholic Christianity — Catholic beliefs — Papers 1, 2 and 3

Creation

Guided 1 Outline **three** Catholic beliefs about Creation.

Catholics believe that God created the world.

A second belief is ....

....

....

Another belief is ....

....

.... **(3 marks)**

2 Explain **two** reasons why the biblical account of Creation is important for Catholics in understanding the nature of God.

> Remember that you need to give two different reasons. Develop each one fully by adding examples or a full explanation of your point.

....

....

....

....

....

....

....

....

....

.... **(4 marks)**

The significance of the Creation account

1   Outline **three** Catholic beliefs about stewardship.

    ....

    ....

    ....

    > In your answer, you could focus on what stewardship is, examples of how Catholics can put stewardship into action or general beliefs held by Catholics about stewardship.

    ....

    ....

    ....

    ....

    .... **(3 marks)**

2   Explain **two** reasons why Catholics believe humans have a special role within the world.

    ....

    ....

    ....

    > To answer this question successfully, think about how God made humans to be special – for example, that they are made 'in the image of God' (Genesis 1:27), or the duties they were given, such as stewardship and dominion.

    ....

    ....

    ....

    ....

    ....

    .... **(4 marks)**

Had a go ☐   Nearly there ☐   Nailed it! ☐

Catholic Christianity
Catholic beliefs
Papers 1, 2 and 3

The Incarnation

1 Outline **three** Catholic beliefs about Jesus as the incarnate Son.

> In this question, you are required to give three Catholic beliefs about Jesus' life as a human on Earth – think about different aspects of his life and what they mean for Catholics.

....

....

....

....

....

....

....

.... **(3 marks)**

2 Explain **two** reasons why Jesus as the incarnate Son is important for Catholics.

In your answer you must refer to a source of wisdom and authority.

> Think about what Jesus in human form demonstrates about God. Fully explain each reason you give – making sure you develop them both – and link one of your reasons to a quote from a source of authority such as the Bible.

....

....

....

....

....

....

....

....

....

.... **(5 marks)**

Had a go ☐ Nearly there ☐ Nailed it! ☐

Events of the Paschal Mystery

1 Outline **three** Catholic beliefs about the death and resurrection of Jesus.

   ....

   > This question asks you to focus only on the death and resurrection of Jesus – make sure that you don't include any beliefs about the other main events in his life.

   ....

   (3 marks)

2 Explain **two** reasons why the events of the Paschal Mystery are important to Catholics today.

   ....

   > The Paschal Mystery refers to the events of the passion, death and resurrection of Jesus. This is a central belief for Catholics; this question asks you to explain why this is. Make sure that you give two different reasons and develop each one fully.

   ....

   (4 marks)

Had a go ☐   Nearly there ☐   Nailed it! ☐

Jesus' life, death and resurrection

1 Outline **three** Catholic beliefs about the role of Jesus in salvation.

> Salvation refers to the process by which a person is saved from sin through belief in Jesus and God's grace.

....

....

....

....

....

....

....

.... **(3 marks)**

Guided 2 Explain **two** reasons why salvation is important for Catholics today.

Salvation helps to restore the relationship between

God and humanity. ....

> Develop this reason by adding an example to further explain the point being made. Then go on to give a second reason and make sure you develop it by adding new information or an example to show your understanding.

....

....

....

....

....

....

....

.... **(4 marks)**

Had a go ☐ Nearly there ☐ Nailed it! ☐

Eschatology

In this question, 3 of the marks awarded will be for your spelling, punctuation and grammar, and your use of specialist terminology.

1 "Belief in life after death is important today."

Evaluate this statement considering arguments for and against.

In your response you should:

- refer to Catholic teachings
- refer to different Christian points of view
- reach a justified conclusion.

> With an evaluation question like this, it is always a good idea to plan your answer first and to consider what arguments you are going to include. Make sure that you develop every argument and reason you use.

> Remember, there are 3 marks available for spelling, punctuation and grammar (SPaG), so check through your answer carefully.

(15 marks)

Please complete your answer on your own paper if you need more space.

Had a go ☐ Nearly there ☐ Nailed it! ☐

Catholic Christianity
Marriage and the family
Paper 1

Marriage

Guided 1 Outline **three** Catholic beliefs about the importance of marriage for society.

Catholics believe that marriage provides security and so helps to give stability to society. ....

> Add two more beliefs that indicate reasons why marriage is important for society.

....

....

....

....

(3 marks)

2 Explain **two** reasons why Catholics believe marriage is important.

....

....

....

....

....

....

....

(4 marks)

Had a go ☐ Nearly there ☐ Nailed it! ☐

Sexual relationships

1 "Sex should always be saved for marriage."

Evaluate this statement considering arguments for and against.

In your response you should:

- refer to Catholic teachings
- refer to non-religious points of view
- reach a justified conclusion.

> Remember, Catholics believe that sex is a gift from God, which should be kept within marriage in order to create a sacred bond between husband and wife, and for the purpose of procreation. You must show awareness of this in your answer.

> You need to show awareness that other Christians may believe that sex within marriage is special, but see it as a way of expressing love and not just for procreation. Remember that non-religious people may also think that sex is special, but believe that marriage is not as important as religious believers think it is.

> Remember to bring your answer to a close by offering a justified conclusion. This is where you offer your own opinion or draw a final conclusion about all the ideas you included in your answer.

(12 marks)

Please complete your answer on your own paper if you need more space.

Had a go ☐ Nearly there ☐ Nailed it! ☐

Catholic Christianity — Marriage and the family — Paper 1

Families

1. Outline **three** beliefs about the purpose of family for Catholics.

   ....
   ....
   ....
   ....
   ....
   ....
   ....

   > Give three different beliefs, putting each one in a separate sentence. Make sure that you are clear about the reasons you give and that they are sufficiently different. For example, if you say that the purpose of family is 'to bring children up as Christians' and 'to educate children in the religion of Christianity', your answers would be too similar to count as separate reasons.

   (3 marks)

> **Guided**

2. Explain **two** reasons why Catholics believe the family provides security.

   Catholics believe that the family provides a safe and loving environment in which children can be raised and educated. ....

   ....
   ....
   ....
   ....
   ....
   ....

   > Make sure that you give two different reasons and fully develop each one by adding further information or examples.

   (4 marks)

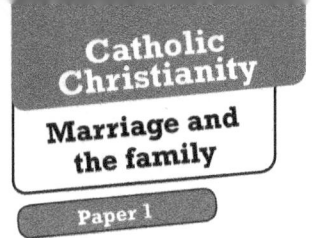

Had a go ☐   Nearly there ☐   Nailed it! ☐

Support for the family in the Catholic parish

Guided

1. Outline **three** ways that the local Catholic parish can help families.

   The local Catholic parish can organise classes or events at which families can meet other families. ....

   > Give two more ideas. Make sure that they are different and present each one in a separate sentence.

   ....

   ....

   .... **(3 marks)**

2. Explain **two** reasons why the local Catholic parish believes it is important to help families.

   > Always read the question carefully – this one asks **why** the parish thinks it is important to help families, not what they do to help.

   ....

   ....

   ....

   ....

   ....

   ....

   .... **(4 marks)**

Had a go ☐   Nearly there ☐   Nailed it! ☐

Catholic Christianity — Marriage and the family — Paper 1

Family planning

1 "Contraception should not be used."

Evaluate this statement considering arguments for and against.

In your response you should:

- refer to Catholic teachings
- refer to non-religious points of view
- reach a justified conclusion.

> Remember that you have to show a range of views in your answer. Include reasons why Catholics may agree with the statement, and reasons why non-religious people may either agree or disagree. Give a justified conclusion after considering all the reasons you include.

(12 marks)

Please complete your answer on your own paper if you need more space.

Catholic Christianity — Marriage and the family — Paper 1

Had a go ☐ Nearly there ☐ Nailed it! ☐

Divorce

Guided 1 Explain **two** reasons why Catholics believe marriage is for life.

Vows are spoken during the marriage ceremony that include the line 'till death us do part'. Marriage is intended to be a lifelong commitment, which the couple agrees to in the vows made to each other and before God. ....

> One reason is given here and developed. You could also include an answer that links to the reason Catholics do not accept divorce – think about why they hold this view.

(4 marks)

2 Explain **two** reasons why Catholics are against remarriage.

In your answer you must refer to a source of wisdom and authority.

> Remember – Catholics believe that marriage is for life. They consider remarriage to be adultery, only accept annulment under extreme circumstances and do not recognise divorce.

(5 marks)

Had a go ☐   Nearly there ☐   Nailed it! ☐

Catholic Christianity
Marriage and the family
Paper 1

Men and women in the family

Guided

1. Outline **three** Catholic teachings about the role of men and women in the family.

   The Bible teaches in Genesis 1:27 that God made both men and women 'in his image', giving them equal and important roles in the family. ....

   ....

   ....

   ....

   ....

   (3 marks)

2. Explain **two** reasons why Catholics believe the roles of men and women are equal in family life.

   > Give your first reason and then develop it by adding an example or new information to explain the point you have made.

   > Give a second reason, making sure it is different to the first. Again, make sure you develop it by adding new information or an example to show your understanding.

   (4 marks)

Gender prejudice and discrimination

1 Outline **three** Catholic beliefs about why gender prejudice and discrimination are wrong.

   > Catholics work to overcome gender prejudice and discrimination – this question asks you to give three separate reasons as to **why** they do this.

   ....

   ....

   ....

   ....

   ....

   ....

   .... **(3 marks)**

2 Explain **two** reasons why Catholics do not accept the ordination of women.

   > Think of two different reasons why Catholics do not believe that women can hold the position of priest in the Church. Link your reasons to Catholic teachings if possible.

   ....

   ....

   ....

   ....

   ....

   ....

   ....

   ....

   .... **(4 marks)**

Had a go ☐   Nearly there ☐   Nailed it! ☐

Sacramental nature of reality

1 Outline **three** sacraments for Catholics.

   ....

   ....

   > Remember that there are seven sacraments – you need to name three of them.

   ....

   ....

   ....

   ....

   ....   **(3 marks)**

Guided 2 Explain **two** reasons why the sacrament of the Eucharist is important to Catholics.

One reason is because the bread and wine used in the

Eucharist represent the body and blood of Jesus. ....

   > Develop each reason: why is Jesus important to Catholics and why is it important for them to remember the Last Supper?

....

....

....

Another reason is because the Eucharist remembers the Last Supper

in the life of Jesus. ....

....

....   **(4 marks)**

Had a go ☐ Nearly there ☐ Nailed it! ☐

Liturgical worship

1 Outline **three** features of Mass for Catholics.

   > State three things that happen as part of the Mass service.

   ....

   ....

   ....

   ....

   ....

   ....

   ....

   .... **(3 marks)**

2 Explain **two** reasons why liturgical worship is important to Catholics.

   > Liturgical worship is a form of worship carried out in public by a group of people and it follows a set pattern.

   ....

   ....

   ....

   ....

   ....

   ....

   ....

   ....

   .... **(4 marks)**

Had a go ☐   Nearly there ☐   Nailed it! ☐

Catholic Christianity — Living the Catholic life — Papers 1, 2 and 3

Liturgy of the funeral rite

1 Outline **three** aims of funeral rites for Catholics.

> Give three reasons why Catholics believe funerals have a purpose.

....

....

....

....

....

....

....

(3 marks)

Guided

2 Explain **two** reasons why funerals are important to Catholics.

In your answer you must refer to a source of wisdom and authority.

Funerals are important as they allow people to say goodbye to the person who has died. ....

> Think about the purpose of funerals as well as what happens during the service. Fully develop each reason you give and add a supporting reference to **one** of the two reasons.

....

....

....

....

....

....

....

....

(5 marks)

Catholic Christianity — Living the Catholic life (Papers 1, 2 and 3)

Had a go ☐   Nearly there ☐   Nailed it! ☐

Prayer

Guided   1   Outline **three** examples of prayer for Catholics.

An example of prayer used by Catholics is the Lord's Prayer. ....

....

....

....

....

....

....

> This type of question does not require you to explain each idea. You just need to give three different examples, each in its own sentence.

(3 marks)

2   Explain **two** reasons why prayer is important for Catholics.

....

....

....

....

....

....

....

....

....

> Give examples of prayers that Catholics use (such as the Lord's Prayer or the Hail Mary prayer) to help you develop the reasons you include.

(4 marks)

Had a go ☐ Nearly there ☐ Nailed it! ☐

Catholic Christianity — Living the Catholic life — Papers 1, 2 and 3

Popular piety

1 Outline **three** features of the Stations of the Cross.

....

....

....

....

....

.... **(3 marks)**

Guided

2 Explain **two** reasons why different types of worship are important for Catholics.

Some forms of worship may be particularly relevant to personal or individual occasions. For these occasions, informal worship may allow an individual to develop a deeper and more personal connection with God. ....

....

....

....

.... **(4 marks)**

> You could mention liturgical (formal) worship, popular piety or individual prayer as examples in your answer. Remember to develop each reason you give with examples.

Had a go ☐ Nearly there ☐ Nailed it! ☐

Pilgrimage

In this question, 3 of the marks awarded will be for your spelling, punctuation and grammar, and your use of specialist terminology.

1 "Pilgrimage is important today."

Evaluate this statement considering arguments for and against.

In your response you should:

- refer to Catholic teachings
- refer to different Christian points of view
- reach a justified conclusion.

> This question asks you to focus on the importance of pilgrimage **today** – be careful that you don't just give general reasons why it is important or discuss the purpose of pilgrimage instead. Remember, some Christians feel that pilgrimage remembers past events that may or may not be relevant today. Show awareness of arguments for and against the statement in your answer.

....
....
....
....
....
....
....
....
....
....
....
....
....
....
....
....
....
....

> Remember, there are 3 extra SPaG marks available for this question, so check your answer carefully.

.... **(15 marks)**

Please complete your answer on your own paper if you need more space.

Had a go ☐   Nearly there ☐   Nailed it! ☐

Catholic Christianity — Living the Catholic life — Papers 1, 2 and 3

Catholic social teaching

1. Outline **three** ways that the charity CAFOD (the Catholic Agency for Overseas Development) puts social teachings into action.

   ....

   ....

   ....

   ....

   ....

   .... **(3 marks)**

Guided

2. Explain **two** reasons why Catholics believe they should help others.

   Catholics believe that they have a duty from God to help others. ....

   > Develop this reason by adding an example or some new information to further explain the point that has been made. Try to give an example of a religious teaching.

   ....

   ....

   ....

   ....

   > Now add a second reason – remember to develop it fully.

   ....

   ....

   ....

   .... **(4 marks)**

Had a go ☐ Nearly there ☐ Nailed it! ☐

Mission and evangelism

Guided 1 Outline **three** ways Catholics carry out missionary work.

Catholics can spread the word of God by sharing the Bible with others. ....

> Give three separate sentences – each one containing a different idea.

....

....

....

....

....

.... **(3 marks)**

2 Explain **two** reasons why missionary work is important to Catholics.

....

....

....

....

....

....

....

.... **(4 marks)**

Had a go ☐ Nearly there ☐ Nailed it! ☐

Catholic Christianity
Matters of life and death
Paper 1

Origins of the universe

> **Guided**

1 Explain **two** Catholic responses to scientific explanations of the universe.

Some Catholics believe that religion and science can work together to explain how the universe came to exist. ....

....

....

Some Catholics believe that scientific explanations and the Bible contradict each other, and would reject scientific explanations about the creation of the universe. ....

....

....

Two responses have been given – add a sentence of further explanation or an example to develop each one.

(4 marks)

> **Guided**

2 Explain **two** reasons why Catholics believe the universe should not be used as a commodity.

Catholics believe that God created the world, which makes it special. It should not be exploited or destroyed as it was God's gift to humanity.

Another reason is ....

....

....

....

This first part of the answer gives a reason, which is then developed through the new information about the world being a gift from God. Add a second reason below and develop it in the same way.

(4 marks)

25

Sanctity of life

Had a go ☐ Nearly there ☐ Nailed it! ☐

Guided 1 Outline **three** reasons why Catholics regard human life as holy.

Human life is holy because God created humans in his own image.

One reason has been outlined. Give two more reasons – each in its own sentence.

....

....

....

....

....

....

(3 marks)

2 Explain **two** reasons why Catholics believe life is special and holy.

....

....

....

....

....

....

....

....

*Questions 1 and 2 use the same content but the **styles** of these questions are different. Make sure that you know how to answer each one correctly. For question 2, make sure that you give two different reasons. Then develop each reason by adding an example or some new information to explain it fully.*

(4 marks)

Had a go ☐   Nearly there ☐   Nailed it! ☐

Catholic Christianity — Matters of life and death — Paper 1

Origins of human life

1 "Catholic beliefs about the origin of human life can be accepted as well as scientific beliefs about evolution."

Evaluate this statement considering arguments for and against.

In your response you should:

- refer to Catholic teachings
- refer to non-religious points of view
- reach a justified conclusion.

> Make sure to offer arguments that both agree and disagree with the statement. Develop each argument fully and use them to come to an overall conclusion.

(12 marks)

Please complete your answer on your own paper if you need more space.

Abortion

1 Explain **two** reasons why Catholics do not accept abortion.

In your answer you must refer to a source of wisdom and authority.

> Reasons why Catholics do not accept abortion might include: the sanctity of life; life begins at conception; God has a purpose for every life; and teachings from the *Humanae Vitae*. Choose two and remember to develop each one, linking **one** reason to a source of wisdom and authority.

....

(5 marks)

2 Explain **two** reasons why some Christians do not accept the Catholic view and do accept abortion.

> Reasons why some Christians may accept abortion include: Jesus' teaching about compassion; in cases such as rape or incest; or if the mother's life is at risk. Choose two reasons and remember to develop each one fully.

....

(4 marks)

Had a go ☐ Nearly there ☐ Nailed it! ☐

Catholic Christianity
Matters of life and death
Paper 1

Life after death

> **Guided**

1. "Everyone should believe in life after death."

   Evaluate this statement considering arguments for and against.

   In your response you should:
   - refer to Catholic teachings
   - refer to non-religious points of view
   - reach a justified conclusion.

   > Make sure that you plan your answer before you start writing. Remember to include Catholic views (using teachings as support) as well as non-religious views. Explain each reason fully before moving on.

   Catholics stress the importance of a belief in the afterlife because it influences how they live their lives. They believe that if they follow Catholic teachings to live a good life and help others, they will be rewarded by eternal life in heaven with God. ....

   (12 marks)

Please complete your answer on your own paper if you need more space.

Non-religious arguments against life after death

1. Outline **three** ways Catholics respond to non-religious arguments against life after death.

   ....

   ....

   ....

   ....

   ....

   ....

   ....

   ....
   (3 marks)

   > Questions 1 and 2 use the same content but have different styles of question. For Question 2, you just need to identify three different ways in which they may respond. For Question 2, you are required to not only give two different responses but explain and expand on each one, giving an example or further information to show your understanding.

2. Explain **two** ways Catholics respond to non-religious arguments against life after death.

   ....

   ....

   ....

   ....

   ....

   ....

   ....

   ....

   ....
   (4 marks)

   > Remember that Catholics do think that a belief in the afterlife is important. It guides how they live their lives on Earth and they feel that sources of authority, such as the Bible or Catholic Church teachings, provide sufficient evidence to support a belief in the afterlife.

Had a go ☐   Nearly there ☐   Nailed it! ☐

Catholic Christianity
Matters of life and death
Paper 1

Euthanasia

Guided

1 Outline **three** Catholic teachings about euthanasia.

Add two more teachings to complete this answer.

The Bible teaching 'You shall not murder' (Exodus 20:13) makes it clear that euthanasia is wrong. ....

....

....

....

....
(3 marks)

2 Explain **two** reasons why Catholics do not accept euthanasia.

Remember that there are Bible teachings that specifically forbid killing, which is how Catholics view euthanasia. Try to use these to support the reasons you give in your answer.

....

....

....

....

....

....

....

....

....

....
(4 marks)

Issues in the natural world

1. "Catholics have a duty not to exploit the world."

   Evaluate this statement considering arguments for and against.

   In your response you should:
   - refer to Catholic teachings
   - refer to the ethical theory of utilitarianism
   - reach a justified conclusion.

   > Make sure that you support the arguments you give with Catholic teachings. Remember to incorporate ideas from the ethical theory of utilitarianism in your answer.

   (12 marks)

   Please complete your answer on your own paper if you need more space.

Had a go ☐   Nearly there ☐   Nailed it! ☐

Catholic Christianity — Crime and punishment — Paper 2

Justice

1. Outline **three** Catholic beliefs about the importance of justice.

   ....
   ....
   ....
   ....
   ....
   .... **(3 marks)**

> **Guided**

2. Explain **two** reasons why Catholics believe justice is important for the victims of crimes.

   Catholics believe that justice is important for the victims of crime because it means the criminal has been made to pay for their crime, usually by being given a fair and appropriate punishment. ....
   ....
   ....

   > Develop this answer by adding an example or some new information to support the point being made. If you can, link it to a teaching or key Catholic belief about the idea of justice.

   Catholics believe that it is important for victims of crime (and the rest of society) to feel safe and protected.

   > Develop the second reason in the same way as the first.

   ....
   ....
   .... **(4 marks)**

Had a go ☐ Nearly there ☐ Nailed it! ☐

Crime

Guided 1 Explain **two** ways Catholics may respond to the problem of crime in society.

One way may be to reduce the causes of crime and to prevent people becoming involved in crime. ……………

……………………………………………………………………

……………………………………………………………………

……………………………………………………………………

> A response has been given and needs to be developed. Try to relate the example given to Catholic beliefs or teachings about why they work to reduce the causes of crime.

Another way is to work to help those who have committed crimes and to support them as they go back into society.

……………………………………………………………………

……………………………………………………………………

……………………………………………………………………

> A second response has been given but, as before, it needs to be developed.

(4 marks)

2 Explain **two** reasons why Catholics believe it is important to work to end crime.

In your answer you must refer to a source of wisdom and authority.

…………………………………………………………………………

…………………………………………………………………………

…………………………………………………………………………

…………………………………………………………………………

…………………………………………………………………………

> Think about the following: Catholics believe that no one is free from sin; there are many teachings in the Bible and from the Catholic Church about helping others and working to achieve a better society; Catholics believe they will be judged after death on the way that they have acted in their lives. Make sure that you develop each reason and link **one** of them to a source of authority.

…………………………………………………………………………

…………………………………………………………………………

…………………………………………………………………………

…………………………………………………………………………

…………………………………………………………………………

…………………………………………………………………………

(5 marks)

Had a go ☐   Nearly there ☐   Nailed it! ☐

Catholic Christianity — Crime and punishment — Paper 2

Good, evil and suffering

1 "Suffering comes from God."

Evaluate this statement considering arguments for and against.

In your response you should:
- refer to Catholic teachings
- refer to non-religious points of view
- reach a justified conclusion.

....

(12 marks)

Please complete your answer on your own paper if you need more space.

Punishment

Had a go ☐ Nearly there ☐ Nailed it! ☐

1 Outline **three** Catholic beliefs about why criminals deserve to be punished.

....

....

....

....

....

....

....

> Catholics believe that punishment is important when crimes have been committed. You are being asked to think about **why** this is. Remember that Catholics have key teachings about justice.

(3 marks)

> Guided

2 Explain **two** reasons why Catholics would support punishment.

Catholics may agree with Bible teachings such as Luke 12:47, which supports fair and just punishment for wrongdoing. ....

....

....

....

....

....

....

....

> Complete the explanation of this reason by developing it. You could add a sentence with new information to expand on the point given, provide an example, or give an explanation of what Luke 12:47 says. You then need to add a second different reason and develop it in the same way.

(4 marks)

Had a go ☐ Nearly there ☐ Nailed it! ☐

Catholic Christianity
Crime and punishment
Paper 2

Aims of punishment

1 "The most important aim of punishment is to protect society."

Evaluate this statement considering arguments for and against.

In your response you should:

- refer to Catholic teachings
- reach a justified conclusion.

> Remember that there are a number of aims of punishment. Protection and retribution are two of them — other aims include deterrence and reform. Show awareness of all of these aims in your answer and explain why Catholics may believe that some are more important than others.

....

> At the end of your answer, you are expected to reach a justified conclusion.

....

(12 marks)

Please complete your answer on your own paper if you need more space.

Had a go ☐ **Nearly there** ☐ **Nailed it!** ☐

Forgiveness

1. Outline **three** Catholic teachings about forgiveness.

   ....

   ....

   ....

   ....

   ....

   ....

   .... **(3 marks)**

   > Make sure that you give three different Catholic teachings – each one in a separate sentence.

Guided 2. Explain **two** reasons why Catholics believe it is important to show mercy towards criminals.

Catholics believe that as God shows mercy towards them, they should show mercy towards others, including criminals. ....

....

....

....

Catholics follow Bible teachings about being merciful towards others, which they try to apply to their own lives. ....

....

....

.... **(4 marks)**

> Develop the first reason by expanding on why mercy is important. Develop the second reason by giving an example of a Bible teaching about mercy – you could consider the teachings of Jesus.

Had a go ☐ Nearly there ☐ Nailed it! ☐

Catholic Christianity — Crime and punishment — Paper 2

Treatment of criminals

1 "Criminals should have human rights."

Evaluate this statement considering arguments for and against.

In your response you should:

- refer to Catholic teachings
- refer to relevant ethical arguments
- reach a justified conclusion.

> You need to include Catholic teachings in your answer – think about using your knowledge of Proverbs 31:8–9. You must also include relevant ethical arguments, such as what situation ethics may say about this statement. Remember to reach a justified conclusion at the end, in which you bring together all of your arguments.

....

(12 marks)

Please complete your answer on your own paper if you need more space.

Had a go ☐   Nearly there ☐   Nailed it! ☐

Capital punishment

1. Explain **two** reasons why some Catholics may support the death penalty.

   Make sure that you give two different reasons and develop each one fully.

   ....

   (4 marks)

2. Explain **two** reasons why some Catholics may oppose the death penalty.

   In your answer you must refer to a source of wisdom and authority.

   *You need to give two different reasons and to develop each one fully. You also need to link **one** of your reasons to a quote from a source of authority such as the Bible or Catholic Church Catechism.*

   ....

   (5 marks)

Had a go ☐   Nearly there ☐   Nailed it! ☐

Catholic Christianity
Peace and conflict
Paper 2

Peace

Guided   1 Outline **three** ways that Jesus is recognised as a peacemaker.

Jesus is called the 'Prince of Peace'. ....

....

....

....

....

....

(3 marks)

2 Explain **two** reasons why peace is important for Catholics.

....

....

> Think about Jesus' teachings and how these may relate to ideas of peace.

....

....

....

....

....

....

....

(4 marks)

Had a go ☐ Nearly there ☐ Nailed it! ☐

Peacemaking

Guided 1 Explain **two** reasons why Catholics work for peace.

In your answer you must refer to a source of wisdom and authority.

> Make sure that you fully develop each reason you give and link **one** of them to a source of authority.

Catholics work for peace because they believe that this is a duty given to them by God. ....

....

(5 marks)

2 Explain **two** ways Catholics work to achieve peace.

> Pax Christi is a Catholic organisation that works for peace – you could use this example in your answer.

....

(4 marks)

Had a go ☐ Nearly there ☐ Nailed it! ☐

Catholic Christianity — Peace and conflict — Paper 2

Conflict

1 "Religion can bring peace."

Evaluate this statement considering arguments for and against.

In your response you should:

- refer to Catholic teachings
- refer to non-religious points of view
- reach a justified conclusion.

> Remember that you need to include points that both agree and disagree with the statement. Plan your answer first, carefully considering the best arguments to use and the teachings and evidence that you can include to support them.

....

(12 marks)

Please complete your answer on your own paper if you need more space.

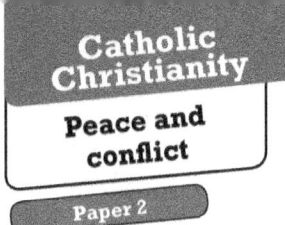

Catholic Christianity — Peace and conflict — Paper 2

Had a go ☐   Nearly there ☐   Nailed it! ☐

Pacifism

1 Outline **three** Catholic teachings on pacifism.

  ....

  ....

  ....

  ....

  ....

  ....

  .... **(3 marks)**

> This questions asks for teachings and not just beliefs – make sure that your answers detail what the religion teaches and not how Catholics may interpret the teachings.

Guided

2 Explain **two** reasons why Catholics may support pacifism.

  There are many Bible teachings from Jesus concerning ideas of peace. ....

  ....

  ....

  ....

  ....

  ....

  ....

  ....

  .... **(4 marks)**

> One reason has been given here. You need to develop it by linking it to a Catholic teaching or example. Then, give a second reason and develop it in the same way.

Had a go ☐ Nearly there ☐ Nailed it! ☐

Catholic Christianity — Peace and conflict — Paper 2

The Just War theory

Guided 1. Outline **three** conditions of Just War theory for Catholics.

One condition is that war must be fought for a just cause. ....

....

....

....

....

Give two more conditions for what makes a war 'just' according to Just War theory.

(3 marks)

2. Explain **two** reasons why some Catholics may believe war can be justified.

....

....

....

....

....

....

....

....

In your answer, you can include arguments related to Just War theory, peace and ideas of justice. Remember to use Catholic teachings to support and develop the arguments you include.

(4 marks)

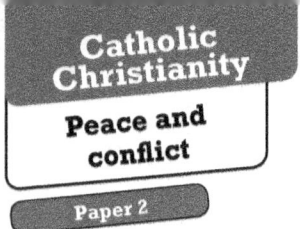

Holy war

1 "Holy war is always wrong."

Evaluate this statement considering arguments for and against.

In your response you should:

- refer to Catholic teachings
- refer to non-religious points of view
- reach a justified conclusion.

> Consider arguments you could use to support the view that any sort of war is wrong. Think about Jesus' teachings on peace, Catechism teachings on the importance of avoiding war and the value of human life. Also consider reasons why non-religious people may consider war to be wrong.

> Now consider arguments you could use to support the idea that holy war may be justified. Catholics may argue that war as a last resort could be justified or in situations where war is the only way to bring about peace. Non-religious people may argue that war could be justified nowadays against threats such as terrorism.

> Finally, offer a full and justified conclusion, considering all the arguments you have presented.

(12 marks)

Please complete your answer on your own paper if you need more space.

Had a go ☐ Nearly there ☐ Nailed it! ☐

Catholic Christianity — Peace and conflict — Paper 2

Weapons of mass destruction

Guided

1. Outline **three** Catholic views on the problems of using weapons of mass destruction.

   Weapons of mass destruction cause too much damage to God's creation. ....

   ....

   ....

   ....

   .... **(3 marks)**

   > Add two more Catholic views – state each one in a separate sentence to make them clear.

2. Explain **two** reasons why Catholics believe the problems of weapons of mass destruction outweigh any possible benefits.

   ....

   ....

   ....

   ....

   ....

   ....

   ....

   .... **(4 marks)**

   > Make sure that you offer two different reasons and develop each one by giving new information or an example to show your understanding.

Catholic Christianity — Peace and conflict — Paper 2

Had a go ☐   Nearly there ☐   Nailed it! ☐

Issues surrounding conflict

1 Explain **two** reasons why Catholics believe conflict is wrong.

In your answer you must refer to a source of wisdom and authority.

....

....

....

....

....

....

....

....

....

....

(5 marks)

Guided

2 Explain **two** ways Catholics have worked to overcome issues of conflict within the world.

Dorothy Day was a Catholic who campaigned against social injustice and conflict in the world.

....

....

> Use examples such as Dorothy Day or Oscar Romero in your answer. You can also use general examples of ways that individual Catholics can work to overcome conflict.

....

....

....

....

....

(4 marks)

Had a go ☐   Nearly there ☐   Nailed it! ☐

Catholic Christianity
Philosophy of religion
Paper 3

Revelation

1 Outline **three** characteristics of God as shown through the revelation of Jesus for Catholics.

> Give three different ideas about God that are shown through the revelation of Jesus (e.g. his omnipotence).

....

....

....

....

....

....

....

(3 marks)

Guided

2 Explain **two** reasons why the revelation of God through Jesus is important to Catholics.

Jesus is believed to be the Son of God and is the second part of the Trinity. ....

....

....

....

> This answer gives one reason explaining the importance of Jesus as a form of revelation but it needs to be developed. You then need to add a second – different – reason and develop it in the same way.

....

....

....

....

(4 marks)

Catholic Christianity — Philosophy of religion — Paper 3

Had a go ☐ Nearly there ☐ Nailed it! ☐

Visions (1)

Guided

1 Outline **three** examples of visions for Catholics.

Saint Bernadette saw a vision of the Virgin Mary.

....

....

....

....

.... **(3 marks)**

2 Explain **two** reasons why visions are important to Catholics.

> Make sure that the reasons you give are different and develop each one fully.

....

....

....

....

....

....

....

....

.... **(4 marks)**

Had a go ☐   Nearly there ☐   Nailed it! ☐

Catholic Christianity — Philosophy of religion — Paper 3

Visions (2)

1 "Visions are good evidence of God's existence."

Evaluate this statement considering arguments for and against.

In your response you should:

- refer to Catholic teachings
- refer to non-religious points of view
- reach a justified conclusion.

> Non-religious people may consider visions to be hallucinations and therefore not proof of God's existence. In your answer, make sure that you present their views as well as Catholic responses to these ideas. Remember that some Catholics will place great emphasis on visions as proof of the existence of God, while others, although recognising that they occur, would rather look to the Bible or Jesus for better evidence. You need to show awareness of all these views in your answer.

(12 marks)

Please complete your answer on your own paper if you need more space.

Miracles

Had a go ☐ Nearly there ☐ Nailed it! ☐

1 "Miracles are proof of God's existence."

Evaluate this statement considering arguments for and against.

In your response you should:

- refer to Catholic teachings
- refer to non-religious points of view
- reach a justified conclusion.

> Plan your answer to this question. Create a list of arguments that both agree and disagree with the statement, making sure that you consider Catholic teachings. Remember that Catholics may hold different views about the importance of miracles.

> Consider which of the arguments you have presented offers the strongest point of view – this will help you to write a reasoned conclusion.

(12 marks)

Please complete your answer on your own paper if you need more space.

Had a go ☐ Nearly there ☐ Nailed it! ☐

Catholic Christianity — Philosophy of religion — Paper 3

Religious experiences

1 Outline **three** Catholic attitudes towards religious experiences.

....

....

....

....

....

....

....

> Remember that some Catholics place great importance on religious experiences and others do not – you can include both of these ideas in your answer.

(3 marks)

2 Explain **two** ways Catholics respond to arguments that religious experiences are NOT proof of God's existence.

....

....

....

....

....

....

....

....

....

....

> Non-religious people may offer arguments such as a lack of scientific evidence, the use of stimulants, hallucinations and wish fulfilment to deny the value of religious experiences. Your task is to explain how Catholics may respond to these arguments.

(4 marks)

Had a go ☐ Nearly there ☐ Nailed it! ☐

The design argument

Guided 1 "The design argument proves there is a God."

Evaluate this statement considering arguments for and against.

In your response you should:

- refer to Catholic teachings.
- refer to non-religious points of view
- reach a justified conclusion.

> A series of suggested arguments that agree and disagree with the statement have been given – each one needs to be developed with further explanation or an example.

The design argument successfully proves God's existence for Catholics because it confirms the faith they already have. ....

....

Another reason why Catholics support the design argument is that they can use it to respond to criticisms such as evolution being the explanation for design in the world, not God. ....

....

A final reason why Catholics agree with the design argument is that there is lots of evidence in the world to support the claims it makes about God being the designer. ....

....

However, non-religious people would not agree with the statement as they believe that evolution is the explanation for design in the world, not God. ....

Furthermore, there is evidence of bad design in the world. ....

....

A final argument is that even if we accept that there is a 'designer' of the world, we cannot prove that it is God. ....

> Having considered all of the arguments presented, you need to write a well-reasoned and comprehensive conclusion.

....

....

....

....

....

(12 marks)

Please complete your answer on your own paper if you need more space.

Had a go ☐   Nearly there ☐   Nailed it! ☐

The cosmological argument

Guided

1. Outline **three** ideas the cosmological argument reveals about the nature of God for Catholics.

   It shows that God is the creator of the universe. ....

   ....

   ....

   ....

   ....

   ....

   ....   **(3 marks)**

   > Add two more characteristics of God revealed by the cosmological argument.

2. Explain **two** reasons why Catholics use the cosmological argument to prove God's existence.

   ....

   ....

   ....

   ....

   ....

   ....

   ....

   ....

   ....   **(4 marks)**

   > You need two different reasons. Make sure that you fully develop each reason in your explanation.

Had a go ☐ Nearly there ☐ Nailed it! ☐

The existence of suffering

Guided

1. Explain **two** reasons why the problem of suffering may raise issues for Catholics.

   Suffering may make Catholics question the nature of God.

   ....

   The presence of suffering in the world challenges both the nature of God and the fact of his existence. Use these ideas in your answer and try to include examples to develop the reasons you give.

   (4 marks)

2. Explain **two** ways in which suffering could affect the faith of a Catholic.

   ....

   (4 marks)

Had a go ☐ Nearly there ☐ Nailed it! ☐

Catholic Christianity — Philosophy of religion — Paper 3

Solutions to the problem of suffering

1. Explain **two** reasons why Catholics believe suffering has a purpose in today's world.

   In your answer you must refer to a source of wisdom and authority.

   > Remember that the Catholic faith offers explanations for why people suffer, so draw on your knowledge of this, as well as how Catholics believe a person should cope when faced with suffering.

   ....

   (5 marks)

Guided

2. Explain **two** ways in which Catholics believe they should respond to the problem of suffering.

   Catholics could respond through prayer. Praying to God can bring hope and comfort for those who are suffering. ....

   ....

   (4 marks)

Catholic Christianity — Equality — Paper 3

Had a go ☐   Nearly there ☐   Nailed it! ☐

Human rights

Guided 1 Explain **two** reasons why Catholics believe they should support human rights.

Catholics believe that all humans are created by God and so deserve to have human rights.

> This first reason needs to be developed. You will then need to add a second developed reason to complete this answer.

....

....

....

....

....

....

.... **(4 marks)**

Guided 2 Explain **two** reasons why Catholics believe human rights are important.

In your answer you must refer to a source of wisdom and authority.

Catholics believe that there are many teachings in the Bible that uphold the idea of human rights. ....

> The answer to this question will include the same Catholic beliefs and teachings as question 1, but the question is worded slightly differently. You also need to link one of your reasons to a source of wisdom and authority, such as the Bible or the Catechism.

....

....

....

Catholics also believe that all humans deserve fair and just treatment because God himself is just. ....

....

....

.... **(5 marks)**

Had a go ☐   Nearly there ☐   Nailed it! ☐

Catholic Christianity — Equality — Paper 3

Equality

1 "Religion can help to achieve equality."

Evaluate this statement considering arguments for and against.

In your response you should:

- refer to Catholic teachings
- reach a justified conclusion.

> To answer this question successfully, you need to be able to explain Catholic beliefs and teachings, and consider what other Catholic beliefs may be seen as more or equally important.

(12 marks)

Please complete your answer on your own paper if you need more space.

Religious freedom

Guided 1. Outline **three** benefits for Catholics of living in a multifaith society.

A multifaith society will have greater religious tolerance.

> Both of these questions require you to state **three** separate ideas. Put each one in a separate sentence and remember that you are not required to explain 'outline' questions, simply to state them.

....

....

....

....

....

.... **(3 marks)**

2. Outline **three** challenges for Catholics of living in a multifaith society.

....

....

....

....

....

.... **(3 marks)**

Had a go ☐ Nearly there ☐ Nailed it! ☐

Religious prejudice and discrimination

1 Explain **two** Catholic attitudes to religious freedom.

In your answer you must refer to a source of wisdom and authority.

.... Start your answer by giving the first attitude. Think about how God created all humans, the importance of equality, teachings about agape love and teachings from the Catechism.

.... Develop your answer by adding an example or new information to help explain the attitude.

.... Quote from a source of wisdom or authority, such as the Bible or Catechism – make sure this is directly linked to the attitude you have given.

.... Give and fully develop a second attitude to complete your answer.

(5 marks)

Catholic Christianity — Equality — Paper 3

Had a go ☐   Nearly there ☐   Nailed it! ☐

Racial harmony

1 Outline **three** reasons why Catholics work for racial harmony.

   ....

   ....

   ....

   ....

   ....

   ....

   (3 marks)

Guided

2 Explain **two** ways in which Catholics have worked for racial harmony.

   Individual Catholic Church leaders are from many ethnic backgrounds and promote racial harmony. ....

   ....

   ....

   ....

   The Catholic Church encourages equality, tolerance and respect. ....

   ....

   ....

   (4 marks)

> Remember that you can use specific examples to answer this question – for example, the Catholic Association for Racial Justice (CARJ) – but you can also include examples of how individual Catholics may work for racial harmony. Develop each of the reasons given.

Had a go ☐ Nearly there ☐ Nailed it! ☐

Catholic Christianity

Equality

Racial discrimination

Paper 3

1 Outline **three** problems for Catholics caused by racial discrimination in society.

....

....

....

....

....

....

....

> Racial discrimination is where a person is treated unfairly because of their race. Consider the impact of this on different racial groups.

(3 marks)

2 Explain **two** reasons why Catholics believe racism is wrong.

....

....

....

....

....

....

....

....

....

> Make sure that you offer two different reasons. Fully develop each one, using examples or teachings where possible.

(4 marks)

Social justice

Guided 1. Outline **three** ways that Catholics work for social justice.

Catholics can organise food banks in their local communities to help those in need. ....

.... **(3 marks)**

2. Explain **two** reasons why Catholics believe they should work for social justice in the world.

> Make sure that you base your answer on what Catholics are taught.

.... **(4 marks)**

Had a go ☐   Nearly there ☐   Nailed it! ☐

Catholic Christianity

Equality

Paper 3

Wealth and poverty

1 "Inequality is the cause of all social injustice in the world."

Evaluate this statement considering arguments for and against.

In your response you should:

- refer to Catholic teachings
- reach a justified conclusion.

> Think about why Catholics may agree or disagree with this statement. Make sure that you fully develop each argument you include, using examples and teachings where possible.

(12 marks)

Please complete your answer on your own paper if you need more space.

Islam

Muslim beliefs

Papers 1, 2 and 3

Had a go ☐ Nearly there ☐ Nailed it! ☐

The Six Beliefs of Islam

Guided 1 Outline **three** features of the Six Beliefs of Sunni Islam.

One feature of the Six Beliefs of Sunni Islam is belief in one God.

Another feature is belief in angels. ....

....

....

....

> This answer has identified two of the Six Beliefs. Add a third belief to complete the answer.

(3 marks)

Guided 2 Explain **two** reasons why the Six Beliefs are important to Sunni Muslims.

The Six Beliefs help all Sunni Muslims to better understand their religion, Islam. For example, ...

....

....

> Two reasons have been given in this answer. Develop each one by adding a suitable example from your knowledge of the Six Beliefs.

Another reason is that the Six Beliefs show Sunni Muslims how to live their lives according to Allah's rules. For example, ...

....

....

....

(4 marks)

Had a go ☐ Nearly there ☐ Nailed it! ☐

Islam — Muslim beliefs — Papers 1, 2 and 3

The five roots of 'Usul ad-Din in Shi'a Islam

1. Explain **two** reasons why Tawhid is important to Muslims.

   ....
   ....
   ....
   ....
   ....
   ....
   ....
   ....
   ....

   > There are many possible reasons including: the five roots of 'Usul ad-Din are all based on the central idea of one God; 'Islam' means 'submission to Allah'; Muslims are aware of Allah in all their actions and direct their daily prayers towards him. Use these (or any other ideas you have) to answer this question successfully.

   (4 marks)

2. Explain **two** of the five roots of 'Usul ad-Din.

   ....
   ....
   ....
   ....
   ....
   ....
   ....
   ....
   ....

   > The five roots are: Tawhid (oneness of Allah), Adl (divine justice), Nubuwwah (prophethood), Imamah (successors to Muhammad) and Mi'ad (Day of Judgement and the Resurrection). Remember that they are only accepted by Shi'a Muslims and are different from the Six Beliefs accepted by Sunni Muslims – be careful not to get them mixed up!

   (4 marks)

Islam — Muslim beliefs (Papers 1, 2 and 3)

Had a go ☐   Nearly there ☐   Nailed it! ☐

The nature of Allah

Guided 1 Outline **three** Muslim beliefs about the characteristics of Allah.

Muslims believe Allah is transcendent.

....

....

....

....

....

Add two other Muslim beliefs about Allah, putting each idea in a separate sentence.

(3 marks)

2 Explain **two** ways the characteristics of Allah are described in the Qur'an.

In your answer you must refer to a source of wisdom and authority.

....

....

....

....

....

....

....

....

....

....

....

*Remember that you **must** include a reference from a source of wisdom and authority for one of the two ways you explain – this can appear anywhere in your answer.*

(5 marks)

Had a go ☐   Nearly there ☐   Nailed it! ☐

Islam — Muslim beliefs — Papers 1, 2 and 3

Risalah

1 Outline **three** Muslim beliefs about the importance of prophets in Islam.

....

....

....

....

....

.... **(3 marks)**

Guided

2 Explain **two** reasons why Risalah is important in Islam.

Prophets are important in Islam as Allah uses them to communicate with humanity. For example, Ibrahim carried messages from Allah to encourage people to worship God.

....

....

....

....

....

....

.... **(4 marks)**

> This answer has given one reason and then developed it using the example of Ibrahim. You need to give a different second reason and then develop it using another example (e.g. Muhammad).

Islam — Muslim beliefs (Papers 1, 2 and 3)

Had a go ☐   Nearly there ☐   Nailed it! ☐

Muslim holy books

Guided

1. Outline **three** features of the Qur'an.

   The Qur'an was revealed to Muhammad. ....

   ....

   ....

   ....

   ....

   ....

   (3 marks)

   Give two more features of the Qur'an, making sure they are different from the piece of information already given.

2. Explain **two** reasons why the Qur'an is important to Muslims.

   ....

   ....

   ....

   ....

   ....

   ....

   ....

   ....

   (4 marks)

   Make sure that you fully develop each reason you give. Give the reason in one sentence and then add a second sentence that either gives new information about the reason or an example.

Had a go ☐ Nearly there ☐ Nailed it! ☐

Islam — Muslim beliefs (Papers 1, 2 and 3)

Malaikah

In this question, 3 of the marks awarded will be for your spelling, punctuation and grammar, and your use of specialist terminology.

1. "Belief in angels is the most important belief in Islam."

   Evaluate this statement considering arguments for and against.

   In your response you should:
   - refer to Muslim teachings
   - reach a justified conclusion.

   > Remember that Muslims have many key beliefs, including one God (Tawhid), life after death (akhirah) and angels (malaikah). You need to consider a range of arguments about the statement before coming to a justified conclusion.

   (15 marks)

   > Remember that there are 3 extra marks available in this question for spelling, punctuation and grammar (SPaG) and the use of special terms, so check your answer carefully.

Please complete your answer on your own paper if you need more space.

Islam — Muslim beliefs
Papers 1, 2 and 3

Had a go ☐   Nearly there ☐   Nailed it! ☐

Al-Qadr

Guided

1 Outline **three** Muslim beliefs about al-Qadr.

Muslims believe that Allah controls everything. ....

....

....

....

....

.... **(3 marks)**

2 Explain **two** ways in which a belief in al-Qadr affects the lives of Muslims.

> Give your first piece of information to answer this question and then develop it by adding new information or an example in a second sentence. Remember that this development must be linked directly to both the information you have given in your first sentence and the question itself.

> Give your second piece of information and develop it in the same way as your first. Remember that this development should add new information about your chosen reason.

(4 marks)

Had a go ☐ Nearly there ☐ Nailed it! ☐

Islam
Muslim beliefs
Papers 1, 2 and 3

Akhirah

1 Outline **three** Muslim beliefs about akhirah.

   ....

   ....

   ....

   ....

   ....

   ....

   ....

   (3 marks)

   > State three separate ideas held by Muslims about life after death.

2 Explain **two** ways in which Muslim beliefs about the afterlife are similar to the main religious tradition of Great Britain.

   ....

   ....

   ....

   ....

   ....

   ....

   ....

   ....

   ....

   ....

   (4 marks)

   > For this question, it may be worth jotting down some brief ideas about the afterlife that you think are similar for both Muslims and Christians. For example: life is seen as a test; ideas of eternal reward and punishment; the concept of resurrection. Then choose two of these ideas to write about in your answer.

   > This style of question can only be asked in this topic (1.8 Beliefs about the afterlife and their significance) and in topic 3.3 (The practice and significance of worship). You will also only be asked to compare and contrast this content in a (b) style exam question.

Islam — Marriage and the family — Paper 1

Had a go ☐   Nearly there ☐   Nailed it! ☐

Marriage

1 Outline **three** Islamic teachings about marriage.

....

....

....

....

....

....

....

> This question is specifically asking what Islam teaches about marriage – make sure your answer focuses on this.

(3 marks)

Guided

2 Explain **two** reasons why marriage is significant for Muslims.

Marriage is important to Muslims as it is believed to be the correct context in which to have a family. Muslims are expected to get married and to raise their children within the Islamic faith. ....

....

....

....

....

....

....

> You need to give a different second reason to complete this answer. This could be that Allah created men and women for each other to be committed through marriage, that marriage is believed to bring stability to society or that the Qur'an instructs Muslims to marry.

(4 marks)

Had a go ☐ Nearly there ☐ Nailed it! ☐

Islam — Marriage and the family — Paper 1

Sexual relationships

Guided

1. Outline **three** teachings about sexual relationships in Islam.

   Muslims believe sex is an act of worship.

   Islam also teaches ....

   ....

   Another teaching about sexual relationships is ....

   ....

   ....

   (3 marks)

   Give each teaching in a separate sentence and on a separate line.

Guided

2. Explain **two** reasons why Muslims believe sex outside marriage is wrong.

   In your answer you must refer to a source of wisdom and authority.

   Muslims believe that Allah intended sex to take place only within marriage. ....

   ....

   ....

   ....

   ....

   Muslims also believe ....

   ....

   ....

   ....

   ....

   ....

   (5 marks)

   Add a sentence to develop this reason and a reference from a source of wisdom and authority (for example, the Qur'an or Hadith) to support it.

   Add a second reason here, making sure that you fully develop it by giving new information, a quote or an example. Make sure that it answers the question as well as developing the point you have made.

75

Islam — Marriage and the family (Paper 1)

Had a go ☐ Nearly there ☐ Nailed it! ☐

Families

Guided

1 "The most important purpose of family for Muslims is to strengthen the ummah."

Evaluate this statement considering arguments for and against.

In your response you should:

- refer to Muslim teachings
- reach a justified conclusion.

Some Muslims agree with the statement as Muslim families often attend the mosque together. This helps to unite all Muslims as they recognise that they are all praying together at the same time each day. Individual family units can feel that they have support and are part of the worldwide ummah through this shared worship. ....

....

....

....

> Remember that the ummah is the worldwide family of Muslims – the nation. Consider reasons that agree and disagree with the idea that this is the most important purpose of the family in Islam.
>
> Begin your answer by considering why some Muslims may agree with this statement. Make sure that you fully develop each reason you give – you could use Islamic teachings or examples to illustrate the points you make.

A reason to disagree with the statement could be ....

....

....

....

....

....

....

....

....

....

....

> Next consider why some Muslims may disagree with the statement – think about what other purposes the family has in Islam in order to come up with reasons.

> Finally, after considering all of your reasons, give a justified conclusion on the statement.

(12 marks)

Please complete your answer on your own paper if you need more space.

Had a go ☐   Nearly there ☐   Nailed it! ☐

Islam — Marriage and the family — Paper 1

The family in the ummah

1. Outline **three** Islamic reasons why it is important for the ummah to provide support to the family.

   ....

   ....

   ....

   ....

   ....

   ....

   ....

   (3 marks)

   > This question focuses on **why** the ummah provides support, not what support they provide.

2. Explain **two** ways in which the ummah can support families.

   ....

   ....

   ....

   ....

   ....

   ....

   ....

   ....

   ....

   (4 marks)

   > Make sure that you give two different reasons and develop each one fully by adding new information or examples.

Had a go ☐ Nearly there ☐ Nailed it! ☐

Contraception

1 "Muslims should not use contraception."

Evaluate this statement considering arguments for and against.

In your response you should:

- refer to Muslim teachings
- refer to different Muslim points of view
- reach a justified conclusion.

> Remember that this question requires you to include Muslim teachings – think about what the different sources of wisdom and authority teach. Muslims do not all hold the same views, so remember to show awareness of this in your answer before you reach a justified conclusion at the end.

....

(12 marks)

Please complete your answer on your own paper if you need more space.

Had a go ☐   Nearly there ☐   Nailed it! ☐

Islam
Marriage and the family
Paper 1

Divorce

1 Explain **two** reasons why some Muslims believe divorce is wrong.

   ....
   ....
   ....
   ....
   ....
   ....
   ....
   ....
   ....

   (4 marks)

> Remember that Muslims believe marriage is important and should be for life as this is what Allah intended. You can use this idea to help you think of two separate reasons.

> Remember that while these two questions seem similar and may refer to similar content, although used differently to answer each question, question 2 requires you to refer to a source of wisdom or authority for one of the two reasons given in your answer.

2 Explain **two** reasons why some Muslims may accept divorce.

   In your answer you must refer to a source of wisdom and authority.

   ....
   ....
   ....
   ....
   ....
   ....
   ....
   ....
   ....
   ....

   (5 marks)

Had a go ☐ Nearly there ☐ Nailed it! ☐

Men and women in the family

1 "Muslim men and women have equal roles in the family."

Evaluate this statement considering arguments for and against.

In your response you should:

- refer to Muslim teachings
- refer to different Muslim points of view
- reach a justified conclusion.

....

(12 marks)

Please complete your answer on your own paper if you need more space.

Had a go ☐ Nearly there ☐ Nailed it! ☐

Islam — Marriage and the family — Paper 1

Gender prejudice and discrimination

Guided 1 Outline **three** examples of how Muslims work for gender equality.

Malala Yousafzai stood up against the Taliban to achieve equality in education. ....

....

....

....

....

....

> State two more examples of things that Muslims have done to work for equality between men and women.

(3 marks)

Guided 2 Explain **two** reasons why Muslims believe gender prejudice and discrimination are wrong.

Islam teaches that men and women should be treated the same way. ....

....

....

....

Muslims believe that after death Allah will judge men and women in the same way. ....

....

....

....

> Two reasons have been given in this answer. Develop each idea by giving some new information or an example for each one.

(4 marks)

Islam — Living the Muslim life (Papers 1, 2 and 3)

Had a go ☐   Nearly there ☐   Nailed it! ☐

The Ten Obligatory Acts of Shi'a Islam

Guided 1 Outline **three** purposes of the Ten Obligatory Acts for Shi'a Muslims.

Shi'a Muslims believe that one purpose is to guide them in how they live their lives.

....

....

....

....

....

> Give a total of three separate purposes and make sure that they are all different.

(3 marks)

Guided 2 Explain **two** ways in which Shi'a Muslims practise the Ten Obligatory Acts.

Shi'a Muslims must pray five times a day as one of the Ten Obligatory Acts. ....

....

....

....

....

> This partial answer has given two ways in which Shi'a Muslims practise the Ten Obligatory Acts – you need to develop each idea by adding an example or new information.

Muslims try to resist temptations that may challenge them in their daily lives. ....

....

....

....

(4 marks)

Had a go ☐   Nearly there ☐   Nailed it! ☐

Islam — Living the Muslim life — Papers 1, 2 and 3

The Shahadah

1. Outline **three** reasons why the Shahadah is significant to Muslims.

   ....

   ....

   ....

   ....

   ....

   .... **(3 marks)**

Guided

2. Explain **two** ways in which the Shahadah is shown to be important for Muslims today.

   The Shahadah is whispered into the ears of newborn babies. This shows it is important because ....

   ....

   ....

   ....

   ....

   ....

   ....

   ....

   .... **(4 marks)**

> To help you answer this question, consider when the Shahadah is spoken: daily; in the ear of a newborn baby; just before death; and recited aloud in front of witnesses.

83

Salah

In this question, 3 of the marks awarded will be for your spelling, punctuation and grammar, and your use of specialist terminology.

1 "Salah is the most important of the Five Pillars for Muslims."

Evaluate this statement considering arguments for and against.

In your response you should:

- refer to Muslim teachings
- reach a justified conclusion.

....

> First, consider arguments that **agree** with the statement, making sure that you develop each one. Think about the regularity of prayer and the fact that it is communication with Allah, which is important to Muslims.

> Next, consider arguments that **disagree** with the statement. Again, make sure they are developed and linked to Muslim teachings. Consider why many Muslims believe Shahadah is more important and, perhaps, the central pillar.

> Finally, after considering all of the arguments, give an overall conclusion. Make sure you make reasoned judgements based on the evidence you have given in your answer.
>
> Remember that there are also 3 marks available in this question for SPaG and special terms – so check your answer through carefully.

(15 marks)

Please complete your answer on your own paper if you need more space.

Had a go ☐   Nearly there ☐   Nailed it! ☐

Islam — Living the Muslim life (Papers 1, 2 and 3)

Sawm

Guided

1. Outline **three** examples of people who may be excused from fasting during Sawm.

   Muslims who are sick may be excused from fasting.

   ....

   ....

   ....

   ....

   ....

   Give two more examples – each one in a different sentence.

   (3 marks)

2. Explain **two** reasons why Sawm is important to Muslims.

   ....

   ....

   ....

   ....

   ....

   ....

   ....

   ....

   Remember to state each reason and then develop it by giving an example, a quote or some new information about the reason. Ensure that your developed reason answers the question and provides more explanation.

   (4 marks)

Islam
Living the Muslim life
Papers 1, 2 and 3

Had a go ☐   Nearly there ☐   Nailed it! ☐

Zakah and khums

Guided

1   Outline **three** features of Zakah for Muslims.

Zakah is 2.5 per cent of a Muslim's annual wealth.

....

....

....

....

....

> These features can include any ideas about Zakah.

(3 marks)

2   Explain **two** reasons why khums is important for Shi'a Muslims.

....

....

....

....

....

....

....

....

> Think about each of the following ideas when forming your reasons: khums is used to help the descendants of Muhammad and leaders of the Shi'a faith; it is a duty; it is one of the Ten Obligatory Acts for Shi'a Muslims.

(4 marks)

Had a go ☐   Nearly there ☐   Nailed it! ☐

Islam — Living the Muslim life (Papers 1, 2 and 3)

Hajj

In this question, 3 of the marks awarded will be for your spelling, punctuation and grammar, and your use of specialist terminology.

1 "The benefits of attending Hajj outweigh the challenges."

Evaluate this statement considering arguments for and against.

In your response you should:

- refer to Muslim teachings
- reach a justified conclusion.

> Think about the benefits and challenges of Hajj to help you create arguments that agree and disagree with the statement.

....

(15 marks)

Please complete your answer on your own paper if you need more space.

Islam — Living the Muslim life
Papers 1, 2 and 3

Had a go ☐   Nearly there ☐   Nailed it! ☐

Jihad

1 Outline **three** features of greater jihad.

....

....

....

....

....

....

....

> This question is asking you to give three examples of the ways a Muslim can perform greater jihad. Remember: this is a personal daily struggle to be a better Muslim and to overcome evil.

(3 marks)

Guided **2** Explain **two** ways in which jihad is understood by Muslims.

Jihad can be interpreted as greater jihad. ....

....

> Develop each idea given in this partial answer.

....

....

....

Jihad can be interpreted as lesser jihad. ....

....

....

....

....

(4 marks)

Had a go ☐ Nearly there ☐ Nailed it! ☐

Islam
Living the Muslim life
Papers 1, 2 and 3

Celebrations and commemorations

In this question, 3 of the marks awarded will be for your spelling, punctuation and grammar, and your use of specialist terminology.

1 "Celebrating festivals such as Id-ul Adha is vital in Islam."

Evaluate this statement considering arguments for and against.

In your response you should:
- refer to Muslim teachings
- reach a justified conclusion.

> With an evaluation question like this, it is always a good idea to plan your answer first. Consider what arguments might be used to agree and disagree with the statement.

....

(15 marks)

Please complete your answer on your own paper if you need more space.

Islam — Matters of life and death — Paper 1

Had a go ☐ Nearly there ☐ Nailed it! ☐

Origins of the universe

1 Outline **three** Muslims teachings about the origins of the universe.

*Write down three **separate** Muslim teachings about how the universe was created.*

....

....

....

....

....

....

....

(3 marks)

Guided

2 Explain **two** Muslim responses to scientific explanations about the universe.

Some Muslims believe that science and Islam together explain how the universe was created.

One partial response has been given – add a further sentence, example or quote to develop the point that has been made. Then add a second response and develop it in the same way.

....

....

....

....

....

....

....

(4 marks)

Had a go ☐ Nearly there ☐ Nailed it! ☐

Islam — Matters of life and death — Paper 1

Sanctity of life

1 Outline **three** Muslim teachings about the sanctity of life.

....

....

....

....

....

....

(3 marks)

Guided

2 Explain **two** reasons why Muslims believe human life is holy.

Muslims believe human life is holy because it was created by Allah. They believe it should be respected as it was made to be sacred.

> One reason has already been given and developed through explanation. Add and develop a second reason in the same way.

....

....

....

....

....

....

(4 marks)

Islam
Matters of life and death — Paper 1

Had a go ☐   Nearly there ☐   Nailed it! ☐

The origins of human life

1. "It is possible to accept both evolution and Islamic ideas about the origin of human life."

   Evaluate this statement considering arguments for and against.

   In your response you should:
   - refer to Muslim teachings
   - reach a justified conclusion.

   > Remember that some Muslims will agree with this statement and others will disagree. You need to show awareness of the reasons for each view in your answer. Think about giving one side of the debate first, then the other, before using the arguments you have included to come to an overall conclusion at the end.

   ....

   (12 marks)

Please complete your answer on your own paper if you need more space.

Had a go ☐　Nearly there ☐　Nailed it! ☐

Islam — Matters of life and death — Paper 1

Muslim attitudes to abortion

1. Explain **two** reasons why some Muslims will not accept abortion.

   > Give two different reasons, making sure that you fully develop your explanation of each one by adding new information, a quote or an example.

   ....

   (4 marks)

2. Explain **two** Muslim responses to arguments that abortion is acceptable.

   ....

   (4 marks)

Islam — Matters of life and death — Paper 1

Had a go ☐   Nearly there ☐   Nailed it! ☐

Death and the afterlife (1)

1. Explain **two** reasons why Muslims support a belief in life after death.

   ....

   ....

   ....

   ....

   ....

   ....

   ....

   .... **(4 marks)**

2. Explain **two** Muslim teachings that support a belief in life after death.

   In your answer you must refer to a source of wisdom and authority.

   > This question asks specifically for you to focus on Islamic teachings and not generic beliefs.

   ....

   ....

   ....

   ....

   ....

   ....

   ....

   ....

   ....

   .... **(5 marks)**

Had a go ☐   Nearly there ☐   Nailed it! ☐

Islam
Matters of life and death
Paper 1

Death and the afterlife (2)

1 "Everyone should believe in life after death."

Evaluate this statement considering arguments for and against.

In your response you should:

- refer to Muslim teachings
- refer to non-religious points of view
- reach a justified conclusion.

> Make sure that you explain why Muslims believe so strongly in life after death – think of what their sources of authority teach them. Consider also why non-religious people do not generally accept a belief in life after death. You may want to show how Muslims respond to these beliefs in your answer.

....
....
....
....
....
....
....
....
....
....
....
....
....
....
....
....
....
....
....
....
....
....
....

(12 marks)

Please complete your answer on your own paper if you need more space.

Islam
Matters of life and death
Paper 1

Had a go ☐   Nearly there ☐   Nailed it! ☐

Euthanasia

1 Outline **three** Muslim teachings against euthanasia.

> Read the question carefully – it focuses specifically on **why** Muslims believe euthanasia is wrong.

....

....

....

....

....

....

....

(3 marks)

Guided

2 Explain **two** reasons why Muslims do not accept euthanasia.

In your answer you must refer to a source of wisdom and authority.

Muslims do not accept euthanasia because they believe in the sanctity of life. The Qur'an teaches 'And do not kill yourselves (or one another)' (Surah 4:29). This shows that life is special and sacred as it was created by Allah and, therefore, should not be ended by humans. ....

> One reason has already been given and developed, and includes a quote from a source of authority and wisdom for Muslims. What other quotes could have been used to support this answer? Add a second developed reason to complete the answer.

....

....

....

....

....

....

....

(5 marks)

Had a go ☐   Nearly there ☐   Nailed it! ☐

Islam — Matters of life and death — Paper 1

Issues in the natural world

1 "Muslims should protect animals."

Evaluate this statement considering arguments for and against.

In your response you should:

- refer to Muslim teachings
- refer to different Muslim points of view
- reach a justified conclusion.

> With an evaluation question like this, it is always a good idea to plan your answer first. Make sure that you show why Muslims may hold differing views about this statement.

....

(12 marks)

Please complete your answer on your own paper if you need more space.

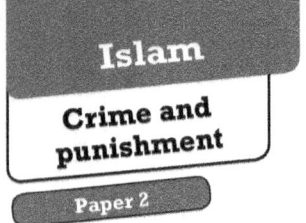

Had a go ☐ Nearly there ☐ Nailed it! ☐

Justice

1 "Justice is important for the victims of crime."

Evaluate this statement considering arguments for and against.

In your response you should:

- refer to Muslim teachings
- reach a justified conclusion.

> To answer this question, think about everyone who benefits from justice being achieved – victims, criminals, society in general, etc.

....

(12 marks)

Please complete your answer on your own paper if you need more space.

Had a go ☐ Nearly there ☐ Nailed it! ☐

Islam — Crime and punishment — Paper 2

Crime

1. Outline **three** Muslim teachings about crime.

   ....

   ....

   ....

   ....

   ....

   .... **(3 marks)**

2. Explain **two** ways Muslim organisations work to end crime.

   > Consider the work done by Muslim organisations such as the Muslim Chaplains' Association or Mosaic. Make sure that you specifically focus on what they **do**, giving examples to support your points.

   ....

   ....

   ....

   ....

   ....

   ....

   ....

   ....

   ....

   .... **(4 marks)**

Islam — Crime and punishment — Paper 2

Had a go ☐   Nearly there ☐   Nailed it! ☐

Good, evil and suffering

1 Outline **three** Muslim teachings about good actions being rewarded.

   ....

   ....

   ....

   ....

   ....

   .... **(3 marks)**

2 Explain **two** reasons why Muslims believe there is suffering in the world.

   > Make sure that the two reasons you give are different. Consider including some of the following beliefs: suffering is part of Allah's plan; suffering is a test of faith; some good can come from suffering; suffering is a reminder of sin; suffering is an opportunity to better understand the nature of God.

   ....

   ....

   ....

   ....

   ....

   ....

   ....

   ....

   .... **(4 marks)**

Had a go ☐ Nearly there ☐ Nailed it! ☐

Islam — Crime and punishment — Paper 2

Punishment

> **Guided**

1. Explain **two** reasons why Muslims may view punishment as a form of justice.

   In your answer you must refer to a source of wisdom and authority.

   [Consider why justice is important to Muslims.]

   Muslims believe that justice in the form of fair punishment is important when crimes have been committed. This is a key idea taught in the Qur'an ....

   [Develop this reason by giving a quote from Surah 2, making sure you explain it in the context of the reason given.]

   ....

   ....

   ....

   Muslims also believe that the ummah requires stability in society, which can be achieved through just punishment when a crime has been committed. ....

   [Develop this second reason in the same way as the first.]

   ....

   ....

   ....

   ....

   (5 marks)

   *[You need to link **one** of your reasons to an Islamic source of authority and wisdom. Consider how you could do this for either of the reasons given. Remember that the source can be used anywhere in your answer.]*

Aims of punishment

1 Outline **three** Qur'anic teachings about punishment.

....

....

....

....

....

....

....

(3 marks)

> Focus on what the Qur'an teaches about punishment – put each teaching in a separate sentence.

2 Explain **two** reasons why the reformation of criminals is important to Muslims.

....

....

....

....

....

....

....

....

(4 marks)

> Remember that there are many aims of punishment, but you must direct your answer to the reformation of criminals as stated in the question.

Had a go ☐   Nearly there ☐   Nailed it! ☐

Islam
Crime and punishment
Paper 2

Forgiveness

1 "Criminals should always be forgiven."

Evaluate this statement considering arguments for and against.

In your response you should:

- refer to Muslim teachings
- reach a justified conclusion.

> Islam teaches about the importance of forgiveness in sources of wisdom and authority such as the Qur'an and Hadith. Think about quoting or paraphrasing ideas from these sources to support your arguments.

....

(12 marks)

Please complete your answer on your own paper if you need more space.

Islam
Crime and punishment
Paper 2

Had a go ☐ Nearly there ☐ Nailed it! ☐

Treatment of criminals

Guided

1 Outline **three** Muslim attitudes about how criminals should be treated.

Muslims believe criminals should be treated with justice.

....

....

....

....

....

....

> Add two more Muslim attitudes about the treatment of criminals to answer this question.

(3 marks)

2 Explain **two** reasons why Muslims believe prisoners' human rights should be protected.

....

....

....

....

....

....

....

....

> Think about what human rights prisoners should have – even though they have done wrong. They cannot have full human rights (e.g. their freedom has been removed), but there are reasons why basic human rights, such as the right to food and water, should be upheld.

(4 marks)

Had a go ☐   Nearly there ☐   Nailed it! ☐

Islam — Crime and punishment — Paper 2

The death penalty

1. "Everyone should support the use of the death penalty."

   Evaluate this statement considering arguments for and against.

   In your response you should:
   - refer to Muslim teachings
   - refer to non-religious points of view
   - reach a justified conclusion.

   > Muslims may agree or disagree with this statement, so include both sides of the debate in your answer. Make sure that you also use Islamic teachings to support the arguments you include. Consider what arguments non-religious people might use to support their opinions. Make sure that you include a reasoned conclusion at the end of your answer.

   (12 marks)

Please complete your answer on your own paper if you need more space.

Islam — Peace and conflict — Paper 2

Had a go ☐   Nearly there ☐   Nailed it! ☐

Peace

1. Outline **three** ways in which Islam is understood as a religion of peace.

   ....

   ....

   ....

   ....

   ....

   ....

   ....

   > Give three specific examples that show why Islam is a peaceful religion. Think about what 'Islam' means, what the Qur'an teaches and how Muslims demonstrate ideas of peace in their daily lives.

   (3 marks)

Guided

2. Explain **two** reasons why peace is important to Muslims.

   The Qur'an teaches the importance of using 'words of peace' (Surah 25:63). ....

   ....

   ....

   ....

   All Muslims are part of the ummah, which unites them in peace. ....

   ....

   ....

   ....

   ....

   > Each of these reasons needs development. Add an example, a quote or further information to explain each point.

   (4 marks)

Had a go ☐　Nearly there ☐　Nailed it! ☐

Islam — Peace and conflict — Paper 2

Peacemaking

1. Explain **two** ways Muslims work for peace.

   ....

   ....

   ....

   ....

   ....

   ....

   ....

   ....

   ....

   (4 marks)

   > Think about the work done by organisations such as Islamic Relief or the Muslim Peace Fellowship as well as how individual Muslims can work for peace.

2. Explain **two** reasons why Muslims believe it is important to work for peace.

   ....

   ....

   ....

   ....

   ....

   ....

   ....

   ....

   ....

   (4 marks)

   > To help you answer this question, you could consider the teachings of Islam, what they teach and why they are important for Muslims.

Islam — Peace and conflict — Paper 2

Had a go ☐   Nearly there ☐   Nailed it! ☐

Conflict

Guided

1 Outline **three** ways Muslims respond to conflict.

Muslims work to bring peace to groups in conflict.

Add two more examples of what Muslims do to deal with conflict situations. State each one in its own sentence.

(3 marks)

2 Explain **two** Muslim teachings on conflict.

In your answer you must refer to a source of wisdom and authority.

*Remember that **one** of your reasons needs to be linked to a source of wisdom and authority such as the Qur'an.*

(5 marks)

Had a go ☐ Nearly there ☐ Nailed it! ☐

Islam — Peace and conflict — Paper 2

Pacifism

Guided

1. "Muslims should all be pacifists."

   Evaluate this statement considering arguments for and against.

   In your response you should:
   - refer to Muslim teachings
   - refer to different Muslim points of view
   - reach a justified conclusion.

   Some Muslims may agree with this statement, believing that Islam is a religion of peace and that putting this into practice in the world can best be done through being pacifist. There are many teachings on peace in the Qur'an, showing that violence is not the answer. ....

   ....

   .... *Continue to develop this section of the answer by giving other reasons in support of the statement.*

   ....

   Some Muslims may disagree with this statement as Islam is not traditionally associated with pacifism. ....

   .... *Continue to develop this section of the answer by giving arguments that do not support the statement.*

   ....

   ....

   ....

   ....

   ....

   .... *Bring your answer to a reasoned conclusion – consider all of the reasons you have presented.*

   ....

   ....

   ....

   (12 marks)

   Please complete your answer on your own paper if you need more space.

Islam — Peace and conflict — Paper 2

Had a go ☐   Nearly there ☐   Nailed it! ☐

The Just War theory

1 Outline **three** Muslim conditions of Just War theory.

   ....
   ....
   ....
   ....
   ....
   ....
   .... **(3 marks)**

> The Just War theory covers the criteria and conditions that must be met in order to make acceptable and to justify the decision to go to war. You are required to give three examples of these.

2 Explain **two** ways Muslims respond to Just War theory.

   ....
   ....
   ....
   ....
   ....
   ....
   ....
   ....
   ....
   .... **(4 marks)**

> Remember that Muslims may respond differently to the Just War theory. Some will support it and recognise it as an option of last resort, while others may reject it altogether. Shi'a Muslims attach importance to this theory as it is one of the Ten Obligatory Acts, whereas Sunni Muslims view it as having less significance.

Had a go ☐ Nearly there ☐ Nailed it! ☐

Islam
Peace and conflict
Paper 2

Holy war

Guided

1 Outline **three** Muslim teachings about war.

The Qur'an suggests that violence can be used if necessary.

Add two more Islamic teachings about war.

....

....

....

....

....

(3 marks)

2 Explain **two** reasons why some Muslims accept holy war.

....

....

....

....

....

....

....

(4 marks)

Weapons of mass destruction

Islam — Peace and conflict — Paper 2

Had a go ☐   Nearly there ☐   Nailed it! ☐

1 "Weapons of mass destruction should never be used."

Evaluate this statement considering arguments for and against.

In your response you should:

- refer to Muslim teachings
- refer to relevant ethical theories
- reach a justified conclusion.

> Remember to ensure you include all aspects required by this question. This includes Muslim teachings and reference to ethical theories such as utilitarianism.

....

(12 marks)

Please complete your answer on your own paper if you need more space.

Had a go ☐   Nearly there ☐   Nailed it! ☐

Islam — Peace and conflict — Paper 2

Issues surrounding conflict

Guided

1 Outline **three** ways Muslims work to reduce conflict.

The Muslim Council of Britain runs education programmes.

....

....

Give two more examples of how Muslims or Muslim groups can work for peace in the world.

....

....

....

.... **(3 marks)**

2 Explain **two** ways Muslims respond to conflict.

....

....

....

You could include one response where Muslims work to reduce conflict – giving specific examples – and one where they may support the use of conflict.

....

....

....

....

....

.... **(4 marks)**

Revelation

Had a go ☐ **Nearly there** ☐ **Nailed it!** ☐

Guided

1. Outline **three** Muslim beliefs about the Qur'an as a form of revelation of Allah.

   Muslims believe that revelation through the Qur'an shows them what Allah is like. ....

   ....

   ....

   ....

   ....

   ....

   (3 marks)

   Think about how Muslims believe revelation happens, what their main source of revelation is, or perhaps what revelation may reveal about Allah.

2. Outline **three** ideas about the nature of Allah shown through revelation in the Qur'an.

   ....

   ....

   ....

   ....

   ....

   ....

   ....

   (3 marks)

   Think about three characteristics of Allah that are shown to Muslims through revelation in the Qur'an.

Had a go ☐ Nearly there ☐ Nailed it! ☐

Islam — Philosophy of religion — Paper 3

Visions

Guided 1 Explain **two** reasons why visions prove the existence of Allah.

Visions show Muslims that Allah is all-powerful and are proof that he exists. ....

....

....

> Develop the first reason given here – perhaps by adding an example or further explanation of how the power of Allah is shown. Then add a second reason and develop it in the same way.

....

....

....

....

....

(4 marks)

2 Explain **two** reasons why Muslims believe visions do not prove Allah exists.

....

....

> Remember that not all Muslims place importance on visions. Identify two reasons why this is and develop each one fully.

....

....

....

....

....

....

....

(4 marks)

Had a go ☐ Nearly there ☐ Nailed it! ☐

Miracles

1 "Miracles are evidence of Allah's existence."

Evaluate this statement considering arguments for and against.

In your response you should:

- refer to Muslim teachings
- refer to non-religious points of view
- reach a justified conclusion.

> Remember that some Muslims place great importance on miracles, while others do not – you need to show awareness of this in your answer. You might also consider including the Muslim response to non-religious views.

....

(12 marks)

Please complete your answer on your own paper if you need more space.

Had a go ☐ Nearly there ☐ Nailed it! ☐

Islam
Philosophy of religion
Paper 3

Religious experiences

1. Outline **three** Muslim beliefs about the nature of religious experiences.

   ....

   ....

   ....

   ....

   ....

   .... **(3 marks)**

> **Guided**

2. Explain **two** reasons why religious experiences are important to Muslims.

   Religious experiences reveal the nature of Allah.
   Muslims believe that Allah's power is shown by
   revealing himself to prophets such as Muhammad.

   > The first part of this answer gives a reason and then successfully develops it, giving more information. To complete this answer, add a second reason and develop it in the same way.

   ....

   ....

   ....

   ....

   ....

   ....

   ....

   ....

   .... **(4 marks)**

The design argument

1 Outline **three** characteristics of Allah revealed by the design argument.

....

....

....

....

....

.... **(3 marks)**

2 Explain **two** ways in which Muslims may respond to the idea that the design argument does not prove the existence of Allah.

> Make sure that you give two different ways and develop each idea fully.

....

....

....

....

....

....

....

.... **(4 marks)**

Had a go ☐ Nearly there ☐ Nailed it! ☐

Islam — Philosophy of religion — Paper 3

The cosmological argument

1. Explain **two** characteristics revealed about the nature of Allah through the cosmological argument.

   > A characteristic is what Muslims believe Allah is like. You need to identify two of these and link them to how the cosmological argument demonstrates that this is what Allah is like.

   ....

   (4 marks)

2. Explain **two** reasons why the cosmological argument is proof that Allah exists.

   ....

   (4 marks)

Islam — Philosophy of religion (Paper 3)

Had a go ☐   Nearly there ☐   Nailed it! ☐

The existence of suffering

1. Outline **three** problems the existence of suffering may raise about Allah for Muslims.

   > Think about the characteristics of Allah that are challenged by the existence of evil and suffering.

   ....

   ....

   ....

   ....

   ....

   ....

   (3 marks)

Guided

2. Explain **two** reasons why suffering may cause people to question their belief in Allah.

   Suffering may make people question their belief in Allah as they may ask why Allah doesn't use his power to prevent suffering. ....

   > Develop this reason by adding an example, a quote or some new information. You then need to give a second reason and develop it in the same way.

   ....

   ....

   ....

   ....

   ....

   ....

   (4 marks)

Had a go ☐   Nearly there ☐   Nailed it! ☐

Islam — Philosophy of religion — Paper 3

Solutions to the problem of suffering

Guided 1. Explain **two** practical ways in which Muslims respond to the existence of suffering.

Some Muslims may respond by helping out with a charity that tries to relieve people's suffering. ....

....

....

....

....

Another response could be for Muslims to pray for those who are suffering. ....

....

....

....

....

> Develop each point given by adding an example, a quote or some new information to fully explain each idea.

(4 marks)

2. Explain **two** Muslim teachings about coping with suffering.

In your answer you must refer to a source of wisdom and authority.

> Make sure that you provide a quote for one of the two teachings you include.

....

....

....

....

....

....

....

....

....

(5 marks)

Human rights

Islam — Equality — Paper 3

Had a go ☐ Nearly there ☐ Nailed it! ☐

1 "Muslims should always support human rights."

Evaluate this statement considering arguments for and against.

In your response you should:

- refer to Muslim teachings
- refer to different Muslim points of view
- reach a justified conclusion.

....

*Start your answer by considering reasons why Muslims may **agree** with the statement. Make sure that you develop every point you make.*

*Next, consider why some Muslims may **disagree** with the statement. Give specific examples to support the reasons you offer.*

Finally, after considering all the reasons you have given, present a reasoned conclusion.

(12 marks)

Please complete your answer on your own paper if you need more space.

Had a go ☐ Nearly there ☐ Nailed it! ☐

Islam
Equality
Paper 3

Equality

> **Guided**

1. Outline **three** Muslim practices that show equality.

   One example is Muslims all praying at the same time.

   ....

   ....

   ....

   ....

   ....

   ....

   (3 marks)

   Think of ways in which Muslims try to achieve equality in their religious practices.

2. Explain **two** reasons why Muslims work for equality.

   ....

   ....

   ....

   ....

   ....

   ....

   ....

   ....

   ....

   ....

   (4 marks)

   This question focuses on why Muslims work for equality – use examples or teachings to support the points you include.

Islam

Equality

Paper 3

Had a go ☐   Nearly there ☐   Nailed it! ☐

Religious freedom

1 "Religious freedom is important in a multi-faith society."

Evaluate this statement considering arguments for and against.

In your response you should:

- refer to Muslim teachings
- refer to non-religious points of view
- reach a justified conclusion.

> Make sure you plan which arguments you want to include in your answer. Develop each argument fully, giving evidence or examples to support each one. Review the arguments you included to help you come to a reasoned conclusion at the end of your answer.

(12 marks)

Please complete your answer on your own paper if you need more space.

Had a go ☐ Nearly there ☐ Nailed it! ☐

Islam — Equality — Paper 3

Prejudice and discrimination

1 Explain **two** reasons why Muslims believe prejudice and discrimination are wrong.

In your answer you must refer to a source of wisdom and authority.

> Give your first reason (for example, because it is a key teaching in the Qur'an).

> Develop your reason by explaining the idea more fully – add new information or an example.

> Give your second reason.

> Develop your second reason in the same way as the first one, by adding an example, a quote or some new information.

> Add a quote from a source of wisdom and authority, for example the Qur'an, to **one** of your two reasons. This can be included anywhere in your answer.

(5 marks)

Islam — Equality — Paper 3

Had a go ☐ Nearly there ☐ Nailed it! ☐

Racial harmony

Guided

1 Outline **three** Muslim teachings about racial harmony.

Muhammad taught that all mankind is descended from Adam and Eve.

....

....

....

....

....

(3 marks)

2 Explain **two** reasons why racial harmony is important to Muslims.

> Make sure that you give two different reasons and develop each idea fully.

....

....

....

....

....

....

....

....

(4 marks)

Had a go ☐   Nearly there ☐   Nailed it! ☐

Islam — Equality — Paper 3

Racial discrimination

1 Outline **three** Muslim teachings about racial discrimination.

> Give three teachings from Islam about why it is wrong to treat people from different races differently.

....

....

....

....

....

....

....

(3 marks)

2 Explain **two** reasons Muslims believe racial discrimination is not acceptable.

> Make sure that you give two different reasons and develop each one fully.

....

....

....

....

....

....

....

....

(4 marks)

Islam — Equality — Paper 3

Had a go ☐   Nearly there ☐   Nailed it! ☐

Social justice

Guided 1 Outline **three** reasons why Muslims work for social justice.

Muslims believe that the Qur'an teaches them to help each other. ....

....

....

....

....

.... **(3 marks)**

Guided 2 Explain **two** Muslim teachings about social justice.

Islam teaches that Muslims will be judged by Allah after death on the way they helped others. ....

> Make sure that you develop each of the reasons given.

....

....

....

....

The Qur'an teaches that all humans are equal as they are all Allah's creation. ....

....

....

....

.... **(4 marks)**

Had a go ☐ Nearly there ☐ Nailed it! ☐

Islam

Equality

Paper 3

Wealth and poverty

1. "All Muslims should share their wealth with others."

   Evaluate this statement considering arguments for and against.

   In your response you should:
   - refer to Muslim teachings
   - refer to different Muslim points of view
   - reach a justified conclusion.

   > Think about planning your answer before you write it. Remember to refer to quotes, examples and evidence to support the reasons you give.

   ....

   (12 marks)

Please complete your answer on your own paper if you need more space.

Exam skills

Had a go ☐ Nearly there ☐ Nailed it! ☐

(a) type questions

Please use your own paper to answer these questions.

(a) type questions are worth 3 marks and ask you to outline or state three things. These may be beliefs, teachings, features, responses or something else.

> Remember that to be successful in this type of question, you need to simply give three correct and accurate pieces of information – you are not required to develop or explain them.

1 Outline **three** of the Six Beliefs of Islam for Sunni Muslims. **(3 marks)**

2 Outline **three** Muslim beliefs about the Qur'an. **(3 marks)**

3 Outline **three** ways belief in al-Qadr affects the lives of Muslims. **(3 marks)**

4 Outline **three** Muslim teachings about sexual relationships. **(3 marks)**

5 Outline **three** Muslim beliefs about divorce. **(3 marks)**

6 Outline **three** ways the Shahadah is spoken by Muslims today. **(3 marks)**

7 Outline **three** features of khums. **(3 marks)**

8 Outline **three** ways Muslims celebrate Id-ul Fitr. **(3 marks)**

9 Outline **three** Muslim teachings about why human life is holy. **(3 marks)**

10 Outline **three** ways Muslims can carry out the role of khalifah. **(3 marks)**

11 Outline **three** Muslim beliefs about justice. **(3 marks)**

12 Outline **three** Muslim teachings about punishment. **(3 marks)**

13 Outline **three** ways Muslims can work for peace. **(3 marks)**

14 Outline **three** Muslim beliefs about visions. **(3 marks)**

15 Outline **three** ways Muslims may respond to suffering. **(3 marks)**

16 Outline **three** Muslim teachings about racial harmony. **(3 marks)**

Had a go ☐   Nearly there ☐   Nailed it! ☐   **Exam skills**

(b) type questions

Please use your own paper to answer these questions.

(b) type questions are worth 4 marks and require you to describe or explain two key areas within the Islamic faith. This could include beliefs, teachings, ideas, features, events or ways, to name a few.

> To be successful in this type of question, state two points and then develop each one. This development could be done by adding a second sentence that explains the point you have made, or by adding new information or offering an example. You can also include a relevant quote.

1 Explain **two** of the five roots of 'Usul ad-Din in Shi'a Islam. **(4 marks)**

2 Explain **two** Muslim beliefs about the roles of prophets. **(4 marks)**

3 Describe **two** ways in which beliefs about the afterlife are different for Muslims and Christians. **(4 marks)**

> You must be able to contrast the areas of belief and practice for the topics of the afterlife and worship. This means being able to describe and explain similarities and differences for these topics.

4 Explain **two** reasons why Muslims believe in life after death. **(4 marks)**

5 Explain **two** teachings about the purpose of family in Islam. **(4 marks)**

6 Explain **two** ways the ummah supports the family. **(4 marks)**

7 Explain **two** Muslim teachings about gender prejudice and discrimination. **(4 marks)**

8 Explain **two** purposes of the Ten Obligatory Acts for Shi'a Muslims. **(4 marks)**

9 Explain **two** conditions for declaration of lesser jihad in Islam. **(4 marks)**

10 Explain **two** Muslim beliefs about the origins of the universe. **(4 marks)**

11 Explain **two** Muslim teachings about euthanasia. **(4 marks)**

12 Explain **two** Muslim teachings about forgiveness. **(4 marks)**

13 Explain **two** Muslim beliefs about the use of weapons of mass destruction. **(4 marks)**

14 Explain **two** ways Muslims may respond to challenges to the cosmological argument. **(4 marks)**

15 Explain **two** ways Muslims respond to inequality in the world. **(4 marks)**

Exam skills

Had a go ☐ Nearly there ☐ Nailed it! ☐

(c) type questions

Please use your own paper to answer these questions.

(c) type questions are worth 5 marks and require you to explain key areas within the Islamic faith. This could include beliefs, teachings, ideas, features, events or ways of worship. You also need to add a relevant source of authority for one of the two points given in your answer.

> To be successful when answering this type of question, state two points and then develop each one by adding further new information, an example or a quote. Link in a teaching from a source of wisdom – you are allowed to paraphrase this and it can be part of the point you have made to answer the question.

1. Explain **two** characteristics of Allah shown in the Qur'an.

   In your answer you must refer to a source of wisdom and authority. **(5 marks)**

2. Explain **two** Muslim teachings about marriage.

   In your answer you must refer to a source of wisdom and authority. **(5 marks)**

3. Explain **two** different ways Muslims view the roles of men and women in the family.

   In your answer you must refer to a source of wisdom and authority. **(5 marks)**

4. Explain **two** reasons why Hajj is important for Muslims.

   In your answer you must refer to a source of wisdom and authority. **(5 marks)**

5. Explain **two** Muslim responses to animals being used for experimentation.

   In your answer you must refer to a source of wisdom and authority. **(5 marks)**

6. Explain **two** Muslim teachings about the treatment of criminals.

   In your answer you must refer to a source of wisdom and authority. **(5 marks)**

7. Explain **two** Muslim teachings about war.

   In your answer you must refer to a source of wisdom and authority. **(5 marks)**

8. Explain **two** ways Muslims may respond to the importance of religious experience.

   In your answer you must refer to a source of wisdom and authority. **(5 marks)**

9. Explain **two** Muslim teachings about religious freedom.

   In your answer you must refer to a source of wisdom and authority. **(5 marks)**

Had a go ☐ Nearly there ☐ Nailed it! ☐

Exam skills

(d) type questions

Please use your own paper to answer these questions.

(d) type questions are worth 12 marks and require you to evaluate a stimulus and consider different viewpoints about the significance of a particular aspect of belief.

> There are many requirements of this type of exam question – read the bullet points carefully. Try to give justified reasons that include examples and teachings. You need to use chains of logical reasoning for your arguments – join up your ideas and evidence to reach an overall justified conclusion that is supported by the points you have made.

1 "All Muslims should get married."

   Evaluate this statement considering arguments for and against.

   In your response you should:

   - refer to Muslim teachings
   - refer to non-religious points of view
   - reach a justified conclusion. **(12 marks)**

2 "Greater jihad is more important than lesser jihad."

   Evaluate this statement considering arguments for and against.

   In your response you should:

   - refer to Muslim teachings
   - refer to different Muslim points of view
   - reach a justified conclusion. **(15 marks)**

3 "It is never right to fight."

   Evaluate this statement considering arguments for and against.

   In your response you should:

   - refer to Muslim teachings
   - refer to non-religious points of view
   - reach a justified conclusion. **(12 marks)**

4 "It is wrong for Muslims to be wealthy."

   Evaluate this statement considering arguments for and against.

   In your response you should:

   - refer to Muslim teachings
   - reach a justified conclusion. **(12 marks)**

> On the exam papers, questions 1 and 3 (the units 'Muslim beliefs' and 'Living the Muslim life') have 3 extra marks available for your use of spelling, punctuation and grammar (SPaG), as well as your use of specialist terminology.

Answers

Catholic Christianity

UNIT 1: CATHOLIC BELIEFS

1 The Trinity

1. One mark will be awarded for each point identified up to a maximum of three marks. (3)
   - The Trinity is part of Catholic baptism services when the sign of the cross is made (1).
   - The Trinity is part of Catholic confirmation services when the sign of the cross is made (1).
   - The Trinity is used in the Nicene Creed (1).
   - The Trinity is reflected in the words of hymns that are sung (1).
   - The Trinity is part of the way in which Catholics bless themselves (1).

   Other valid answers will be accepted.

2. One mark will be awarded for providing each reason and a second mark for development of the reason up to a maximum of four marks. One further mark will be awarded for any relevant source of wisdom and authority. (5)
   - The role of the Father shows God as the powerful creator of the world (1). It reminds Catholics of God's nature and his role in creating the world (1). The Nicene Creed describes him as 'maker of heaven and earth, and of all that is, seen and unseen'. (1)
   - It shows God the Father sending his son Jesus to the world in human form (1). Jesus was sent to Earth as the incarnate Son of God to save humankind from the sins of the whole world (1), as stated in the Nicene Creed: 'For us men and for our salvation, he came down from heaven.' (1)
   - It shows the invisible power of God acting within the world through the Holy Spirit (1). It guides and supports humans (1). In the Nicene Creed, the Holy Spirit is 'the giver of life, who proceeds from the Father and the Son.' (1)

   Other valid answers will be accepted.

2 God as a Trinity of persons

1. "Belief in the Trinity is the most important belief for Catholics." In this question, 3 of the marks awarded will be for your spelling, punctuation and grammar, and your use of specialist terminology. Be sure to make your points specific, and refer to teachings and views, as you are instructed. You can support your arguments with biblical or other teachings. Make sure you give balanced views and then draw a conclusion – make sure you say why this is your conclusion. (15)

   Arguments for the statement:
   - The Trinity is crucial in understanding the three parts of God – God as Father, Son and Holy Spirit. It allows Catholics to understand what God is like and to relate to him better.
   - The Trinity plays a central role in Catholic belief and worship. It is a central part of important rites of passage such as baptism or confirmation, and is represented by making the sign of the cross with oil.
   - Belief in the Trinity is at the centre of Catholic beliefs about Jesus and his role in the world. It strengthens Catholics' belief that God is active in their lives through the example of Jesus and the Holy Spirit.

   Arguments against the statement:
   - Although Catholics may recognise the Trinity as important, other beliefs about God's nature may be regarded as equally or more important – for example, his transcendence. God is accepted as a mystery, therefore Catholics believe that they cannot 'know' everything about him and should focus on other key beliefs too.
   - Many other Christians accept the idea of the Trinity but think that beliefs and teachings such as helping others or working to care for the world are more important as they are of more practical use.
   - Other Catholic teachings such as redemption may be considered to be more important than the idea of the Trinity alone. Through an understanding of the redemption of Jesus, Catholics feel they can get closer to and develop a personal relationship with God.

   Other valid answers will be accepted.

3 Creation

1. One mark will be awarded for each point identified up to a maximum of three marks. (3)
   - Catholics believe that God created the world (1).
   - Some Catholics believe that it took God six days to create the universe (1).
   - Some Catholics believe that God rested on the seventh day (1).
   - Catholics believe that God created the universe from nothing (1).
   - Catholics believe that God planned and designed the universe (1).

   Other valid answers will be accepted.

2. One mark will be awarded for providing each reason and a second mark for development of the reason up to a maximum of four marks. (4)
   - The biblical account of Creation shows that God is omnipotent (1). His power is demonstrated by his creation of the world and everything in it, including humans (1).
   - The biblical account of Creation shows that God is eternal (1). He has no beginning or end. He existed before and will continue to exist after the world has ended (1).
   - The biblical account of Creation shows that God is caring and loving (1). He created everything in the world for humans, who were the final part of his creation (1).

   Other valid answers will be accepted.

4 The significance of the Creation account

1. One mark will be awarded for each point identified up to a maximum of three marks. (3)
   - Catholics believe stewardship is a God-given responsibility (1).
   - Catholics believe stewardship is part of God's purpose for humans in the world (1).
   - Catholics believe they should care for the world as God's creation (1).
   - Catholics believe that performing stewardship is a way of showing love and gratitude towards God (1).
   - Catholics believe that they will be accountable to God after death for how they treated his creation (1).

   Other valid answers will be accepted.

2. One mark will be awarded for providing each reason and a second mark for development of the reason up to a maximum of four marks. (4)
   - Humans were made 'in the image of God' (Genesis 1:27) (1). They were made to be different, and are the final and highest part of God's creation (1).
   - Humans were given the responsibility of stewardship from God (1). Catholics believe that this responsibility makes them different from all of God's other creations (1).
   - Humans were given the duty of dominion from God (1). This means that they were given power over the world, which shows that they are special (1).

   Other valid answers will be accepted.

5 The Incarnation

1. One mark will be awarded for each point identified up to a maximum of three marks. (3)
   - It is easier for humans to relate to the idea of Jesus as the incarnate Son (1).
   - Jesus as the incarnate Son shows the divine aspect of God (1).
   - The birth of Jesus fulfilled the prophecy of Christ coming to Earth (1).
   - Jesus as the incarnate Son helps Catholics to better understand the nature of God (1).
   - Jesus as the incarnate Son gives Catholics hope of an afterlife (1).

   Other valid answers will be accepted.

2. One mark will be awarded for providing each reason and a second mark for development of the reason up to a maximum of four marks. One further mark will be awarded for any relevant source of wisdom and authority. (5)
   - The Incarnation gives Catholics hope, as they believe Jesus was sent to be the saviour of the world (1). The resurrection of Jesus proves that there is an afterlife (1): ' "Don't be alarmed," he said. "You are looking for Jesus the Nazarene, who was crucified. He has risen! He is not here." ' (Mark 16:6) (1)
   - Catholics believe that Jesus is one of the three aspects of God (1). This is an idea known as the Trinity and, through Jesus, this allows Catholics to know God better (1): 'Jesus Christ, the only Son of God, eternally begotten of the Father, God from God, Light from Light, true God from true God.' (Nicene Creed) (1)
   - The concept of Jesus being human on Earth fulfils the prophecy given to humanity (1). It shows that God cares for his creation – he sent Jesus as an example of how humans should live their lives (1): 'The Word became flesh and made his dwelling among us. We have seen his glory, the glory of the one and only Son, who came from the Father, full of grace and truth.' (John 1:14) (1)

   Other valid answers will be accepted.

6 Events of the Paschal Mystery

1. One mark will be awarded for each point identified up to a maximum of three marks. (3)
   - Jesus was crucified on the cross (1).
   - Jesus died to save humans from the sins of the world (1).
   - Jesus was resurrected three days after his death (1).
   - Jesus showed himself to his disciples after his resurrection (1).
   - Jesus ascended into heaven after his resurrection (1).

   Other valid answers will be accepted.

2. One mark will be awarded for providing each reason and a second mark for development of the reason up to a maximum of four marks. (4)
   - The events of the Paschal Mystery provide evidence for Catholics of an afterlife and the hope of being with God and Jesus in heaven (1). The Catholic Church Catechism supports this, saying that it was part of God's plan for the world (1).
   - Jesus' death on the cross is accepted by Catholics as necessary in order to save humans from the sins of the whole world (1). It is through Jesus' sacrifice that Catholics believe their sins will be forgiven (1).
   - The events of the Paschal Mystery are a significant part of commemoration and celebration in the Catholic Church (1). They are marked through the festival of Easter (1).

   Other valid answers will be accepted.

7 Jesus' life, death and resurrection

1. One mark will be awarded for each point identified up to a maximum of three marks. (3)
   - Catholics believe that Jesus' sacrifice gives them hope of reward in heaven (1).
   - Jesus was sent to the world to redeem the sins of humanity (1).
   - Jesus was sacrificed through his crucifixion on the cross (1).
   - Those who believe in Jesus can be saved (1).
   - God sent Jesus to restore the relationship between God and humanity (1).

   Other valid answers will be accepted.

2. One mark will be awarded for providing each reason and a second mark for development of the reason up to a maximum of four marks. (4)
   - Salvation helps to restore the relationship between God and humanity (1). This was broken when Adam and Eve disobeyed God in the Garden of Eden (1).
   - Salvation reaffirms the benevolent nature of God for Catholics (1). It demonstrates that God is merciful and will forgive those who try to redeem themselves, cleansing their souls of sin (1).
   - Belief in salvation is important because it gives Catholics hope (1). It provides evidence of an afterlife, which Catholics believe they can achieve through God's grace (1).

   Other valid answers will be accepted.

8 Eschatology

1. "Belief in life after death is important today." In this question, 3 of the marks awarded will be for your spelling, punctuation and grammar, and your use of specialist terminology. Be sure to make your points specific, and refer to teachings and views, as you are instructed. You can support your arguments with biblical or other teachings. Make sure you give balanced views and then draw a conclusion – make sure you say why this is your conclusion. (15)

   Arguments for the statement:
   - Catholics' belief in life after death has a big impact on their lives on Earth. They believe that, after death, God will judge them on the way they have lived and they will then be rewarded or punished in the afterlife; this affects how they live their lives today.
   - The Bible contains key teachings about the afterlife and how God wants Christians to live their lives. Catholics follow these teachings so that they can be rewarded in heaven with God.
   - Catholics believe that Jesus' resurrection proves there is an afterlife and that they should live their lives in the knowledge of this belief. Catholics believe they should follow the example of Jesus, who was perfect and without sin.

   Arguments against the statement:
   - Although Christians accept that the afterlife is important, other beliefs may have equal importance. Catholics and other Christians believe that a belief and faith in God is central to the religion, giving this equal importance.
   - Some Christians place less emphasis on a belief in the afterlife. They may teach that other beliefs, such as helping others and caring for the world, are also important. These actions will naturally lead to a reward in the afterlife.
   - Some Christians may view life as a test for the final judgement and believe that this idea is more important than that of reward or punishment in the afterlife. They may accept that they have been given responsibilities from God that tell them how to live their lives and are therefore more important.

   Other valid answers will be accepted.

UNIT 2: MARRIAGE AND THE FAMILY

9 Marriage

1. One mark will be awarded for each point identified up to a maximum of three marks. (3)
   - Catholics believe that marriage provides security and so gives stability to society (1).
   - Catholics believe that stable relationships within marriage strengthen society (1).

- Catholics believe that, within marriage, children can be educated in the Catholic faith and so contribute to a moral society (1).
- Catholics believe that marriage provides a secure environment in which to raise children to be good members of society (1).
- Catholics believe that marriage provides the basic family unit on which society is founded (1).

Other valid answers will be accepted.

2 One mark will be awarded for providing each reason and a second mark for development of the reason up to a maximum of four marks. (4)
- Marriage is how God intended that men and women should live together (1). God created male and female so they could become 'one flesh' (Mark 10:8) (1).
- Pope Francis taught that marriage was 'not just good but beautiful' (1). He intended to show that men and women complement each other through marriage (1).
- Marriage is seen as the ideal environment in which Catholics can raise a family (1). Catholics believe that they were given a responsibility to have children and to raise them within the Catholic faith (1).

Other valid answers will be accepted.

10 Sexual relationships

1 "Sex should always be saved for marriage." Be sure to make your points specific, and refer to teachings and views, as you are instructed. You can support your arguments with Bible or other teachings. Make sure you give balanced views and then draw a conclusion – make sure you say why this is your conclusion. (12)

Arguments for the statement:
- Catholics believe that sex is a gift from God for the purpose of procreation and should be saved for marriage. This is where a couple can demonstrate their love and commitment to each other, and begin to raise a family.
- The Catholic Church Catechism teaches that marriage is a sacrament before God where sexual relationships should take place: 'Sexuality is ordered to the conjugal love of man and woman. In marriage the physical intimacy of the spouses becomes a sign and pledge of spiritual communion. Marriage bonds between baptised persons are sanctified by the sacrament.' (CCC 2360)
- Catholics may take a vow of chastity, promising not to have a sexual relationship until they are married in order to respect the gift given by God. This demonstrates ideas of purity and the notion of saving themselves until they are committed in marriage.

Arguments against the statement:
- Non-religious people may feel that as long as no one else is hurt, sexual relationships outside marriage are acceptable. They may believe that a sexual relationship is a form of commitment that does not need to be officially recognised by marriage.
- Some Christians believe that another purpose of sex is to deepen the relationship between a man and a woman, and that this can happen prior to marriage if the couple's intention is to get married in the future.
- Non-religious people may not see anything wrong with a sexual relationship prior to marriage, as it is a way of forming a bond between a couple and ensuring that they are compatible.

Other valid answers will be accepted.

11 Families

1 One mark will be awarded for each point identified up to a maximum of three marks. (3)
- Catholics believe that the family is the correct place to raise children (1).
- Catholics believe that the family provides stability and security for children (1).
- Catholics believe that the family allows children to be raised in the correct moral and social environment (1).
- Catholics believe that the family allows children to be introduced to Catholicism (1).
- Catholics believe that the family is how God intended people to live together in society (1).

Other valid answers will be accepted.

2 One mark will be awarded for providing each reason and a second mark for development of the reason up to a maximum of four marks. (4)
- Catholics believe that the family provides a safe and loving environment in which children can be raised and educated (1). They can be taught the difference between right and wrong through the teaching of rules such as the Ten Commandments (1).
- Catholics believe that the family provides a secure environment for children to be introduced to Catholicism (1). They can attend church and worship together as a family (1).
- The Bible teaches the importance of the family unit, as it is how God intended humans to live together (1). It provides a safe and committed setting for a married couple to procreate (1).

Other valid answers will be accepted.

12 Support for the family in the Catholic parish

1 One mark will be awarded for each point identified up to a maximum of three marks. (3)
- The local Catholic parish can organise classes or events at which families can meet other families (1).
- The local Catholic parish can organise parent support classes (1).
- The local Catholic parish will hold family worship services (1).
- The local Catholic parish is involved in rites of passage events for families (1).
- The local Catholic parish offers counselling support for families who are struggling (1).

Other valid answers will be accepted.

2 One mark will be awarded for providing each reason and a second mark for development of the reason up to a maximum of four marks. (4)
- The local Catholic parish believes that helping families is a duty given to them by God (1). Catholics believe they have a duty to help others, especially when they are struggling (1).
- The local Catholic parish believes that the family is at the centre of Catholic beliefs (1). They believe they have a responsibility to educate children in the Catholic faith and to share Christian teachings (1).
- The local Catholic parish believes in supporting the family, as this is how God intended people to live together (1). The celebration of rites of passage or family worship services can help to unite and strengthen the family unit (1).

Other valid answers will be accepted.

13 Family planning

1 "Contraception should not be used." Be sure to make your points specific, and refer to teachings and views, as you are instructed. You can support your arguments with biblical or other teachings. Make sure you give balanced views and then draw a conclusion – make sure you say why this is your conclusion. (12)

Arguments for the statement:
- Catholics believe that it is God's intention for couples to procreate within marriage and the use of contraception prevents this. The first book of the Bible instructs Adam and Eve: 'As for you, be fruitful and increase in number' (Genesis 9:7). This teaches Catholics that procreation is the purpose of sex and so the use of contraception is wrong.
- Catholics believe the *Humanae Vitae* of Pope Paul VI affirms the Catholic belief that artificial contraception is not acceptable. It states: 'The transmission of human

life is a most serious role in which married people collaborate freely and responsibly with God the Creator.' Catholics understand this to mean that the use of artificial contraception is forbidden.
- Catholics believe that contraception could encourage immoral behaviour and promiscuity, which is not how God wants humans to live. The Catholic Church teaches that sexual relationships should only take place within marriage and for the purpose of procreation.

Arguments against the statement:
- Catholics may accept natural forms of contraception rather than artificial methods as this still allows for the possibility of conception. For example, the rhythm method leaves the decision of whether to conceive to God, who has the power to give life.
- Some Catholics follow the teachings of Pope Francis, who amended traditional teachings about the use of contraception stated in the *Humanae Vitae*. His teachings do not promote the use of contraception but state that the use of contraception to prevent the spread of sexually transmitted infections (STIs) is sensible and 'the lesser of two evils'.
- Non-religious people and Humanists may have no ethical objection to using contraception as it is a sensible method of family planning and they are not constrained by religious teachings.

Other valid answers will be accepted.

14 Divorce

1 One mark will be awarded for providing each reason and a second mark for development of the reason up to a maximum of four marks. (4)
- Vows are spoken during the marriage ceremony that include the line 'till death us do part' (1). Marriage is intended to be a lifelong commitment, which the couple agrees to in the vows made to each other and before God. (1)
- Marriage is a sacrament from God and intended to be for life (1). When a couple marries, God becomes part of the marriage and the promises made before him should not be broken (1).
- Jesus spoke out against divorce (1). He reminded Catholics that marriage unites man and woman as 'one flesh' (Mark 10:8) (1).

Other valid answers will be accepted.

2 One mark will be awarded for each reason and a second mark for the development of the reason up to a maximum of four marks. One further mark will be awarded for any relevant source of wisdom and authority. (5)
- Catholics do not believe in divorce, so do not accept remarriage (1). They believe that marriage is intended for life and that this vow should not be broken (1). The couple promise 'till death do us part' (Vows) (1).
- Jesus spoke out against divorce (1). He understood it to be a type of adultery as marriage is intended to be for life (1): 'Anyone who divorces his wife and marries another woman commits adultery against her.' (Mark 10:11) (1)
- The Catholic Church Catechism teaches that divorce and remarriage are wrong (1). Marriage is intended to be for life in order to bring stability to the family unit and society (1): 'Divorce is a grave offence against the natural law. It claims to break the contract, to which the spouses freely consented, to live with each other till death.' (CCC 2384) (1)

Other valid answers will be accepted.

15 Men and women in the family

1 One mark will be awarded for each point identified up to a maximum of three marks. (3)
- The Bible teaches in Genesis 1:27 that God made both men and women 'in his image', giving them equal and important roles in the family (1).
- Some Bible teachings instruct women to obey their husbands (1).
- Genesis 2:18 teaches Catholics that God made woman as a 'helper' for man (1).
- The Bible teaches that men and women were made to have different but complementary roles in the family (1).
- Galatians 3:28 teaches that all Christ's followers, both men and women, are equal and so are equal in the family (1).

Other valid answers will be accepted.

2 One mark will be awarded for providing each reason and a second mark for development of the reason up to a maximum of four marks. (4)
- The Catholic Church Catechism teaches that men and women have roles that are equally important and complement each other in the family (1). It emphasises the contribution of both men and women to the family unit: 'The family is the original cell of social life. It is the natural society in which husband and wife are called to give themselves in love and in the gift of life.' (CCC 2207) (1)
- Catholics accept that all humans are made 'in the image of God' (Genesis 1:27) (1). Although men and women are seen to have different roles within the family, they are of equal worth as both are God's creation (1).
- Catholics believe that there are many Bible teachings promoting the idea of equality between men and women, meaning that their roles within the family are also equal (1). For example: 'There is neither Jew nor Gentile, neither slave nor free, nor is there male and female, for you are all one in Christ Jesus.' (Galatians 3:28) (1)

Other valid answers will be accepted.

16 Gender prejudice and discrimination

1 One mark will be awarded for each point identified up to a maximum of three marks. (3)
- Catholics believe that gender prejudice and discrimination are wrong as all humans are God's creation and so of equal value (1).
- The Catholic Church Catechism teaches that gender prejudice and discrimination are wrong (1).
- Bible teachings suggest that men and women are equal, making gender prejudice and discrimination wrong (1).
- Catholics believe that men and women have different but complementary roles, making gender prejudice and discrimination wrong (1).
- Pope John Paul II taught that gender prejudice and discrimination are wrong (1).

Other valid answers will be accepted.

2 One mark will be awarded for providing each reason and a second mark for development of the reason up to a maximum of four marks. (4)
- Catholics believe that the priest represents Jesus (1). As Jesus was a man, this role cannot be carried out by women (1).
- Catholics teach that men and women were made the same but with different roles (1). This difference means women are not allowed to hold certain positions within the Church that are traditionally held by men (1).
- Women are seen to hold different roles within the Church (1). They can be Ministers of the Eucharist, Altar servers and Readers (1).

Other valid answers will be accepted.

UNIT 3: LIVING THE CATHOLIC LIFE

17 Sacramental nature of reality

1 One mark will be awarded for each point identified up to a maximum of three marks. (3)
- One Catholic sacrament is baptism (1).
- One Catholic sacrament is confirmation (1).
- One Catholic sacrament is marriage (1).
- One Catholic sacrament is ordination or holy orders (1).
- One Catholic sacrament is the Eucharist (1).

Other valid answers will be accepted.

137

2 One mark will be awarded for providing each reason and a second mark for development of the reason up to a maximum of four marks. (4)
- The sacrament of the Eucharist is important for Catholics because the bread and wine used in the ceremony represent the body and blood of Jesus (1). Catholics remember Jesus' sacrifice to save humankind from the sins of the world and to offer the possibility of salvation (1).
- The Eucharist remembers the Last Supper in the life of Jesus (1). This is when Jesus met for the final time with his disciples and gave them instructions on how to remember him after his death (1).
- Catholics believe in transubstantiation – the idea that the bread and wine actually become the body and blood of Jesus (1). They believe that through taking part in the Eucharist they are actually receiving Jesus into their bodies (1).

Other valid answers will be accepted.

18 Liturgical worship

1 One mark will be awarded for each point identified up to a maximum of three marks. (3)
- A feature of Mass is that the priest processes towards the sanctuary (1).
- A feature of Mass is the presentation of the bread and wine (1).
- Music/songs will take place during the Mass service (1).
- During the Mass service, there will be a sermon from the priest (1).
- During the Mass service, there will be Bible readings (1).

Other valid answers will be accepted.

2 One mark will be awarded for providing each reason and a second mark for development of the reason up to a maximum of four marks. (4)
- Catholics believe that liturgical worship brings people closer to God (1). Services such as Mass are structured and allow time for Catholics to focus on the meaning of the sacrament, which affirms their belief in God and Jesus (1).
- Liturgical worship provides focal points for the service (1). For example, the bread and wine in the Mass service remind Catholics of Jesus' sacrifice (1).
- Liturgical worship is a formal way of connecting to God (1). Catholics believe that following the Church's directions for worship is the correct way to show respect and gratitude to God (1).

Other valid answers will be accepted.

19 Liturgy of the funeral rite

1 One mark will be awarded for each point identified up to a maximum of three marks. (3)
- The aim of funeral rites is to say goodbye to the deceased (1).
- The aim of funeral rites is to express the hope of resurrection (1).
- The aim of funeral rites is to show communion with the deceased (1).
- The aim of funeral rites is to unite the Catholic community in prayer (1).
- The aim of funeral rites is to comfort the family of the deceased (1).

Other valid answers will be accepted.

2 One mark will be awarded for each reason and a second mark for development of the reason up to a maximum of four marks. One further mark will be awarded for any relevant source of wisdom and authority. (5)
- Funerals are important as they allow people to say goodbye to the person who has died (1).
Catholics believe in the resurrection of the body and eternal life with God in heaven: (1) 'A farewell to the deceased is his final "commendation to God" by the Church. It is "the last farewell by which the Christian community greets one of its members before his body is brought to its tomb".' (CCC 1690) (1)
- Funerals allow the family time to grieve and to pray for the deceased (1). They are an opportunity to celebrate the life of the deceased, supported by the Church community (1): 'The purpose of the Catholic Funeral Liturgy is to offer worship and thanksgiving to God … to pray for the deceased, and to offer support to the bereaved.' (Guide to preparing for a funeral) (1)
- Catholics believe that the funeral rite represents the communion between the Church on Earth and in heaven (1). The body of the deceased is returned to the Earth, where it is believed to have come from (1): 'for dust you are and to dust you will return.' (Genesis 3:19) (1)

Other valid answers will be accepted.

20 Prayer

1 One mark will be awarded for each point identified up to a maximum of three marks. (3)
- An example of prayer used by Catholics is the Lord's Prayer (1).
- An example of prayers used by Catholics are Mass prayers (1).
- Catholics use the Sign of the Cross prayer in worship (1).
- One form of prayer for Catholics is personal prayer (1).
- An example of a prayer used by Catholics is the Hail Mary prayer (1).

Other valid answers will be accepted.

2 One mark will be awarded for providing each reason and a second mark for development of the reason up to a maximum of four marks. (4)
- Prayer is a form of communication with God and allows Catholics to develop a personal relationship with him (1). Prayers such as the Lord's Prayer contain key beliefs about God's nature, which allows Catholics to understand him better (1).
- Prayer is a way of asking God for help when it is needed (1). Catholics believe that God listens to their prayers and answers them (1).
- The Bible and the Catholic Church Catechism teach that prayer is important (1). It is seen as the raising of a Catholic's heart and mind to God (1).

Other valid answers will be accepted.

21 Popular piety

1 One mark will be awarded for each point identified up to a maximum of three marks. (3)
- There are fourteen Stations of the Cross (1).
- The Stations of the Cross are a series of fourteen images showing Jesus (1).
- The Stations of the Cross remember the suffering of Jesus on the day of his crucifixion (1).
- The Stations of the Cross have particular importance during the festival of Lent (1).
- Each Station of the Cross has its own prayer to be spoken by Catholics (1).

Other valid answers will be accepted.

2 One mark will be awarded for providing each reason and a second mark for development of the reason up to a maximum of four marks. (4)
- Some forms of worship may be particularly relevant to personal or individual occasions (1). For these occasions, informal worship may allow an individual to develop a deeper and more personal connection with God. (1).
- Some forms of worship may provide an important framework for Catholics to celebrate the sacraments (1). The celebration of the Eucharist through the Mass service is liturgical and very structured (1).
- Some forms of worship, such as the Stations of the Cross, help Catholics to remember important religious and historical events (1). The Stations of the Cross help Catholics to remember the significance of Jesus' suffering and sacrifice (1).

Other valid answers will be accepted.

22 Pilgrimage

1. "Pilgrimage is important today." Be sure to make your points specific, and refer to teachings and views, as you are instructed. You can support your arguments with biblical or other teachings. Make sure you give balanced views and then draw a conclusion – make sure you say why this is your conclusion. In this question, 3 of the marks awarded will be for your spelling, punctuation and grammar, and your use of specialist terminology. (15)

   Arguments for the statement:
   - Pilgrimage is important to Catholics today because it gives them the opportunity to visit places of religious and historical importance, and connects them to events from the past. Going to places such as Jerusalem means they can trace the events of the life of Jesus and feel a personal connection to them.
   - Pilgrimage to places such as Vatican City, the centre of the Roman Catholic Church and the place where the pope lives, have special importance for Catholics today. They are able to visit, receive blessings and hear the pope speak, which provides a stronger connection to their religion.
   - Pilgrimage is considered important to Catholics today as it gives them the opportunity to join with other followers and to share in their faith. Catholics believe they can understand their faith better, connect with other Catholics and feel closer to God, as well as strengthening their personal faith.

   Arguments against the statement:
   - Some Christians do not consider pilgrimage to be as important as others do, especially today. They may feel that, while it is important to remember historical religious events, it is more important to live in today's world and to practise the religion on a daily basis than to visit places with historical links to the faith.
   - Some Christians may feel that the money spent on going on a pilgrimage could be put to better use. They may feel that duties from God, such as caring for others, mean that the money could be used in a more practical way in order to make a difference in today's world.
   - There is no duty to complete a pilgrimage in Christianity, so both Catholic and Protestant Christians may feel that it is not an essential part of their religion today. They may feel that pilgrimage is out of date and irrelevant, and they should focus on other more important aspects of their faith.

   Other valid answers will be accepted.

23 Catholic social teaching

1. One mark will be awarded for each point identified up to a maximum of three marks. (3)
   - The Catholic Agency for Overseas Development (CAFOD) works to fight poverty (1).
   - CAFOD tries to make people self-sufficient (1).
   - CAFOD educates people about public health issues (1).
   - CAFOD provides water, food and medical supplies in times of crisis (1).
   - CAFOD speaks out against injustice in the world (1).

   Other valid answers will be accepted.

2. One mark will be awarded for providing each reason and a second mark for development of the reason up to a maximum of four marks. (4)
   - Catholics believe that they have a duty from God to help others (1). This can be seen in Bible teachings such as 'Love your neighbour as yourself'. (Mark 12:31) (1)
   - The Parable of the Sheep and the Goats teaches that those who help others will be rewarded by God (1). Catholics believe that if they help others, this will help them to achieve heaven and be with God in the afterlife (1).
   - Pope Francis has taught through *Evangelii Gaudium* that the Church has a social mission to help others (1). It states that they should help those in poverty and need (1).

   Other valid answers will be accepted.

24 Mission and evangelism

1. One mark will be awarded for each point identified up to a maximum of three marks. (3)
   - Catholics can spread the word of the God by sharing the Bible with others (1).
   - Catholics can fund projects to spread the word of God (1).
   - Mother Teresa lived among the poor and needy to support them in Calcutta (1).
   - Catholics can organise food banks to offer support to those in need (1).
   - Catholics can visit underdeveloped areas and take part in building projects (1).

   Other valid answers will be accepted.

2. One mark will be awarded for providing a reason and a second mark for development of the reason up to a maximum of four marks. (4)
   - Catholics believe that missionary work is important because they believe they are following Jesus' example (1). By sharing their faith and educating others, they are helping to spread Catholicism's message (1).
   - Catholics believe that through missionary work they can help others, which is a duty from God (1). This duty is reinforced by Pope Francis in *Evangelii Gaudium*, an address given to stress the importance of helping others (1).
   - Catholics believe that the Bible teaches them to share their faith with others (1), for example 'He said to them, "Go into all the world and preach the gospel to all creation".' (Mark 16:15) (1)

   Other valid answers will be accepted.

UNIT 4: MATTERS OF LIFE AND DEATH

25 Origins of the universe

1. One mark will be awarded for providing each reason and a second mark for development of the reason up to a maximum of four marks. (4)
   - Some Catholics believe that religion and science can work together to explain how the universe came to exist (1). They may argue that the 'Big Bang' was used by God to create the universe (1).
   - Some Catholics believe that scientific explanations and the Bible contradict each other, and would reject scientific explanations about the creation of the universe (1). As the 'Big Bang' does not require the existence of God, they would argue that only the Bible gives the true explanation, although this has not been Church teaching for some time (1).

   Other valid answers will be accepted.

2. One mark will be awarded for providing each reason and a second mark for development of the reason up to a maximum of four marks. (4)
   - Catholics believe that God created the world, which makes it special (1). It should not be exploited or destroyed as it was God's gift to humanity (1).
   - Catholics believe that God created humans to be stewards of the universe (1). This means that they should be caretakers of the universe, looking after it for future generations and returning it to God unspoiled (1).
   - Catholics believe that, after death, they will be judged on how they have lived their lives on Earth: this includes caring for the universe (1). If they have looked after God's creation it will help them to be rewarded in heaven (1).

   Other valid answers will be accepted.

26 Sanctity of life

1. One mark will be awarded for each point identified up to a maximum of three marks. (3)
   - Catholics believe that human life is holy because God created humans in his own image (1).
   - Catholics believe that human life is holy because God gave humans a soul and so they are different from all of his other creations (1).

- The Bible teaches that people's bodies are temples of the Holy Spirit (1).
- Catholics believe that the Bible story of God breathing life into Adam made him holy (1).
- Bible teachings such as 'You shall not murder' (Exodus 20:13) show that life is holy (1).

Other valid answers will be accepted.

2 One mark will be awarded for providing each reason and a second mark for development of the reason up to a maximum of four marks. (4)
- Catholics believe that God made humans to be different from all other creatures (1). Humans were made 'in the image of God' (Genesis 1:27) (1).
- Catholics believe that all life belongs to God because he created it (1). The Bible teaches that humans should value life and not abuse or take it away (1).
- Catholics believe that God gives each human a soul (1). This is the spiritual part of a human that connects them to God, thus making them special (1).

Other valid answers will be accepted.

27 Origins of human life

1 "Catholic beliefs about the origin of human life can be accepted as well as scientific beliefs about evolution." Be sure to make your points specific, and refer to teachings and views, as you are instructed. You can support your arguments with biblical or other teachings. Make sure you give balanced views and then draw a conclusion – make sure you say why this is your conclusion. (12)

Arguments for the statement:
- Most Catholics see no conflict between evolution and religious teachings, believing that evolution was part of God's plan to create humans. This shows that science and Catholic ideas about the origin of human life can work together to explain how humans came to exist.
- In 2014, Pope Francis made a statement accepting evolution as a part of God's intention to create human beings. If a figure of authority such as the pope sees religion and science as working together, Catholics will be able to follow this teaching.
- Some Catholics believe that the creation of human life is too complex to be explained by either religion or science alone. They believe that science through evolution explains how human life originated, while religion helps Catholics to understand why human life is special, showing how science and religion can work together to provide a full explanation.

Arguments against the statement:
- Some Catholics may hold traditional views about the origin of human life, arguing that the Bible contains the only complete account of how and why it happened. As the Creation story contains no reference to evolution, they would reject any scientific theory and accept only the Bible's explanation of how God alone is responsible for the creation of human life.
- Some Catholics believe that the scientific theory of evolution contradicts religion because it removes the 'special nature' given to humans in the Bible's account. Genesis 1:27 suggests that God planned and designed humans – 'So God created mankind in his own image' – rather than leaving it to chance, as in evolutionary theory.
- Non-religious people may feel that accepting the scientific theory of evolution removes the need to refer to God in order to explain the origin of human life. They would see no reason to include any religious ideas because science offers a full explanation.

Other valid answers will be accepted.

28 Abortion

1 One mark will be awarded for providing each reason and a second mark for development of the reason up to a maximum of four marks. One further mark will be awarded for any relevant source of wisdom and authority. (5)
- Catholics believe that all life was created by God and therefore has value (1). As life begins at conception, abortion is seen as murder, which is forbidden in the Ten Commandments (1): 'You shall not murder.' (Exodus 20:13) (1)
- Catholics believe that God created every human with a plan for their life (1). This means that every human life has a purpose and no other human has the right to end this purpose (1): 'all the days ordained for me were written in your book before one of them came to be.' (Psalm 139:16) (1)
- Pope Paul VI stated in the *Humanae Vitae* that abortion is wrong (1). Catholics believe life is a sacred gift from God and that only God can make decisions about life and death (1): 'all direct abortion, even for therapeutic reasons, [is] to be absolutely excluded as lawful means of regulating the number of children.' (*Humanae Vitae*) (1)

Other valid answers will be accepted.

2 One mark will be awarded for providing each reason and a second mark for development of the reason up to a maximum of four marks. (4)
- Some Christians point to teachings from Jesus, which focus on compassion (1). Sometimes it may be the 'lesser of two evils' for a woman to have an abortion rather than continue with the pregnancy, for example if it results from rape or incest (1).
- All life is sacred, including the life of the mother, so abortion may be allowed if her life is at risk (1). Christians believe that all life deserves protection as it was created by God (1).
- Some Christians may recognise that in cases where a child will be born severely disabled or unlikely to survive, it may be a kinder action to perform an abortion (1). They believe that this would be acting with compassion (1).

Other valid answers will be accepted.

29 Life after death

1 "Everyone should believe in life after death." Be sure to make your points specific, and refer to teachings and views, as you are instructed. You can support your arguments with biblical or other teachings. Make sure you give balanced views and then draw a conclusion – make sure you say why this is your conclusion. (12)

Arguments for the statement:
- Catholics stress the importance of a belief in the afterlife because it influences how they live their lives. They believe that if they follow Catholic teachings to live a good life and help others, they will be rewarded by eternal life in heaven with God.
- Catholics believe that everyone should believe in life after death as the Bible contains important evidence of this. Jesus taught that there was a place in heaven for all when he said 'My father's house has many rooms' (John 14:2), confirming that there is life after death.
- Catholics believe Jesus' resurrection proves that there is life after death. Three days after he was crucified, he was resurrected and revealed himself to his disciples, proving that there is the hope of eternal life for everyone.

Arguments against the statement:
- Non-religious people may believe there is no afterlife and that it is just wishful thinking or a need for comfort that leads us to believe there is. They may think that it gives hope to those who have lost loved ones, but feel that it is a false hope.
- Non-religious people may feel that there is no point in believing in life after death, as there is no actual physical proof of an afterlife. No one has returned or can provide evidence of life after death, so they may instead believe that they should make the most of the one life they have.
- Some non-religious people claim to remember past lives, which they believe to be proof that death is not the end; however, Catholics would not accept that this is good evidence for belief in an afterlife.

Other valid answers will be accepted.

30 Non-religious arguments against life after death

1. One mark will be awarded for each point identified up to a maximum of three marks. (3)
   - Catholics may respond by saying that the resurrection and ascension of Jesus prove there is life after death.
   - Catholics may point to Bible teachings that provide evidence of an afterlife.
   - Catholics may respond by saying that having faith is putting trust in God that there is an afterlife.
   - Catholics may respond by saying that an afterlife gives life on Earth purpose and meaning.
   - Catholics may respond by saying that as God loves his creation he will provide for them after they die.

   Other valid answers will be accepted.

2. One mark will be awarded for providing each way and a second mark for development of the way up to a maximum of four marks. (4)
   - Catholics may respond to non-religious arguments about there being no proof of an afterlife by arguing that there is evidence of life after death through Jesus (1). He was resurrected from the dead and then ascended into heaven, proving that a belief in the afterlife is valid (1).
   - Catholics may respond to the non-religious argument that belief in an afterlife is merely comforting and gives false hope by pointing to teachings in the Bible that provide evidence of an afterlife (1). Jesus said 'My Father's house has many rooms' (John 14:2), offering proof of a life after death.
   - Catholics may respond to non-religious ideas that belief in an afterlife is a way for the Church to exercise control over people by arguing that belief in the afterlife is not about social control but about faith (1). Faith means putting trust in God that Bible teachings of the existence of an afterlife are true (1).

   Other valid answers will be accepted.

31 Euthanasia

1. One mark will be awarded for each point identified up to a maximum of three marks. (3)
   - The Bible teaching 'You shall not murder' (Exodus 20:13) makes it clear that euthanasia is wrong (1).
   - The Catholic teaching that all life is created by God would not permit euthanasia (1).
   - The Catholic teaching that all life has a purpose from God would not permit euthanasia (1).
   - Some Bible accounts teach that suffering may have a purpose, thus making euthanasia wrong (1).
   - The Bible teaching that humans are made 'in the image of God' (Genesis 1:27) would not permit euthanasia (1).

   Other valid answers will be accepted.

2. One mark will be awarded for providing each reason and a second mark for development of the reason up to a maximum of four marks. (4)
   - Human life is a sacred gift from God (1). Catholics believe they were made 'in the image of God' (Genesis 1:27) and that this gift should be protected and not ended prematurely (1).
   - Catholics do not accept murder (1). The Ten Commandments forbid murder and thus the taking of any human life (Exodus 20:13) (1).
   - Many Catholics believe hospices provide an alternative to euthanasia (1). Hospices provide palliative care for those nearing the end of their lives, allowing them to die peacefully and with dignity (1).

   Other valid answers will be accepted.

32 Issues in the natural world

1. "Catholics have a duty not to exploit the world." Be sure to make your points specific, and refer to teachings and views, as you are instructed. You can support your arguments with biblical or other teachings. Make sure you give balanced views and then draw a conclusion – make sure you say why this is your conclusion. (12)

   Arguments for the statement:
   - Catholics believe that God gave them the duty of stewardship. This means that they should care for the world as God's creation and not destroy it.
   - Catholics are taught that the world was given to them as a gift from God. The Bible says 'In the beginning, God created the heavens and the earth' (Genesis 1:1), which suggests that everything ultimately belongs to him and should be cared for.
   - Catholics believe that the world is special because it was given to them as a gift from God. They believe that they will be judged after death on how they cared for the world.

   Arguments against the statement:
   - Catholics believe that although God gave them the duty of stewardship, he also gave them dominion. This means that they have power over the world.
   - Catholic Church teachings state that while Catholics have a duty of stewardship, they can also use the world because it was given to them as a gift. This means that they can use its resources.
   - The ethical theory of utilitarianism proposes that the correct action is to bring about 'the greatest happiness of the greatest number'. According to this principle it is acceptable to use world resources if this benefits humans.

   Other valid answers will be accepted.

UNIT 5: CRIME AND PUNISHMENT

33 Justice

1. One mark will be awarded for each point identified up to a maximum of three marks. (3)
   - Catholics believe God is just and that humans should be too (1).
   - Catholics believe Jesus showed, by example, that everyone should be treated fairly (1).
   - The Catholic Church teaches that justice is important (1).
   - Catholics believe that God will judge them justly after death (1).
   - The biblical prophet Micah taught that God wants people to act justly (1).

   Other valid answers will be accepted.

2. One mark will be awarded for providing each reason and a second mark for development of the reason up to a maximum of four marks. (4)
   - Catholics believe that justice is important for victims of crime because it means the criminal has been made to pay for their crime, usually by being given a fair and appropriate punishment. (1). The Catholic Church follows the teachings of Jesus who promoted ideas of fair treatment for all (1).
   - Catholics believe that it is important for victims of crime (and the rest of society) to feel safe and protected (1). It is important that the victim feels that their crime has been addressed and that the criminal has been dealt with (1).
   - The Bible contains teachings about the importance of God's justice and fair treatment for both criminal and victim (1). It is important for victims to feel that they can trust God to judge wrongdoing after death: 'Do not take revenge ... but leave room for God's wrath, for it is written: "It is mine to avenge; I will repay," says the Lord.' (Romans 12:19) (1)

   Other valid answers will be accepted.

34 Crime

1. One mark will be awarded for providing each way and a second mark for development of the way up to a maximum of four marks. (4)
   - Catholics may work to reduce the causes of crime and to prevent people becoming involved in crime (1). Catholics believe that they have a duty to help others, as shown in the example of Jesus, so they may try to prevent those living in poverty from turning to a life of crime (1).

- Catholics may work to help those who have committed crimes and to support them as they go back into society (1). The Prison Fellowship is a Christian organisation that supports prisoners in order to help them cope with their punishment and to understand why their behaviour was wrong (1).
- Catholics may work with young people to educate them about the effects of crime (1). They may try to raise awareness of the disadvantages of a life of crime in order to help young people live full and happy lives in society.

Other valid answers will be accepted.

2 One mark will be awarded for providing each reason and a second mark for development of the reason up to a maximum of four marks. One further mark will be awarded for any relevant source of wisdom and authority. (5)
- Catholics believe that no one is free from sin and the Bible teaches that we should not judge other people (1). God is believed to be the only one who can judge humans and therefore Catholics believe that they should work to help people – even criminals – and not judge them for their actions (1): 'for all have sinned and fall short of the glory of God.' (Romans 3:23) (1)
- Catholics believe that they have a duty from God to help others (1). They believe that they will be judged after death on their actions and so should help others when given the chance. This includes helping those who may have committed crimes not to reoffend (1): 'If anyone, then, knows the good they ought to do and doesn't do it, it is sin for them.' (James 4:17) (1)
- Catholics believe that justice and fairness are important, and there are many Bible teachings on these topics (1). They believe that God wants them to work to achieve a just society, free from crime (1): 'Listen, you leaders of Jacob, you rulers of Israel. Should you not embrace justice, you who hate good and love evil.' (Micah 3:1–2) (1)

Other valid answers will be accepted.

35 Good, evil and suffering

1 "Suffering comes from God." Be sure to make your points specific, and refer to teachings and views, as you are instructed. You can support your arguments with biblical or other teachings. Make sure you give balanced views and then draw a conclusion – make sure you say why this is your conclusion. (12)

Arguments for the statement:
- Some Catholics will agree that suffering comes from God and view it as a test of their faith. There are examples of this in the Bible, such as in the story of Job. Catholics believe they too are being tested by God on how they cope with suffering in their lives.
- Some Catholics believe that suffering may be the result of God giving humans free will when he created them. They believe that people suffer as a result of their own bad decisions, including the decision to choose evil over good actions.
- Some Catholics may accept that suffering comes from God and has a purpose, but believe that humans do not know what this purpose is. The Bible teaches them to have faith and to put their trust in God in order to help them cope with suffering: 'he will not let you be tempted beyond what you can bear.' (1 Corinthians 10:13)

Arguments against the statement:
- Many non-religious people would not accept that suffering is a test of faith or that it comes from God as they do not believe in a higher divine being. They may argue that the presence of evil and suffering in the world is due to other causes and proves that God does not exist.
- Humanists do not believe that suffering is part of a divine plan from God as they do not believe in a higher being. They may believe that some people suffer through no fault of their own, for example as a result of floods or droughts, which occur naturally.
- Some Christians, including Catholics, may believe that human suffering is a result of people's bad actions and is not due to God. They may refer to teachings such as the Parable of the Sheep and the Goats, which teaches that if people help others and lead good lives they will be judged and rewarded by God in the afterlife, but if they do not they may be punished for their bad actions.

Other valid answers will be accepted.

36 Punishment

1 One mark will be awarded for each point identified up to a maximum of three marks. (3)
- Justice through fair punishment is an important teaching for Catholics (1).
- The Bible describes God as a God of justice (1).
- Catholics believe that God commanded people not to go against their country's laws (1).
- Catholics believe in just punishment as a chance to reform (1).
- Jesus told many parables about fair punishment (1).

Other valid answers will be accepted.

2 One mark will be awarded for providing each reason and a second mark for development of the reason up to a maximum of four marks. (4)
- Catholics may agree with Bible teachings such as Luke 12:47, which supports fair and just punishment for wrongdoing (1). Jesus taught: 'The servant who knows the master's will and does not get ready or does not do what the master wants will be beaten with many blows' (Luke 12:47), suggesting that fair punishment is appropriate (1).
- The Catholic Church teaches that punishment is important when crimes have been committed (1), based on Bible teachings such as 'anyone who does wrong will be repaid for their wrongs.' (Colossians 3:25) (1)
- Catholics believe that God commands them in the Bible to follow the laws of the country in which they live, saying 'Let everyone be subject to the governing authorities' (Romans 13:1) (1). This would include accepting just punishment if they break the law (1).

Other valid answers will be accepted.

37 Aims of punishment

1 "The most important aim of punishment is to protect society." Be sure to make your points specific, and refer to teachings and views, as you are instructed. You can support your arguments with biblical or other teachings. Make sure you give balanced views and then draw a conclusion – make sure you say why this is your conclusion. (12)

Arguments for the statement:
- Catholics would support the protection of society as an important aim of punishment, as they believe that all life is sacred because it is created by God. They would therefore support appropriate punishments for crimes in order to protect people in society from further harm.
- The Catholic Church teaches the importance of the role of justice in protecting victims and the rest of society by making criminals pay for their crimes.
- Some crimes are considered so serious that the main aim of punishment is protecting society, even if this means using capital punishment. For example, some Catholics may support the death penalty for the crime of murder.

Arguments against the statement:
- Some Catholics may feel that when someone has done wrong, the most important Catholic teaching is that of forgiveness rather than punishment. There are many Bible teachings on forgiveness, including Jesus forgiving those who had condemned him to death. Some Catholics believe that they should follow this example in their own lives.
- Some Catholics may believe that the most important aim of punishment is reform, and that this can be achieved by

following the example of Jesus and showing agape love towards those who have done wrong. Giving criminals the chance to understand why their behaviour was wrong and to change so that they can be safely reintegrated back into society may be a better solution for everyone.
- Another equally important aim of punishment is to deter others from committing the same crimes and so to maintain law and order. Catholics follow the Bible teaching of Romans 13:1, which states that people should follow the law of the country in which they live.

Other valid answers will be accepted.

38 Forgiveness

1. One mark will be awarded for each point identified up to a maximum of three marks. (3)
   - The Bible teaches that Jesus died on the cross to bring forgiveness to the world (1).
   - The Catholic Church teaches that Catholics should be forgiving because God is forgiving (1).
   - Prayers such as the Lord's Prayer show that forgiveness is important (1).
   - Luke 6:37 teaches 'Forgive, and you will be forgiven' (1).
   - The Catholic Church teaches that forgiveness is the best way to end conflict (1).

   Other valid answers will be accepted.

2. One mark will be awarded for providing a reason and a second mark for development of the reason up to a maximum of four marks. (4)
   - Catholics believe that as God shows mercy towards them, they should show mercy towards others, including criminals (1). Catholics believe that God helps them to be merciful even when it is difficult (1).
   - Catholics follow Bible teachings about being merciful towards others, which they try to apply to their own lives (1). They believe that they should follow the example of Jesus, who taught 'Blessed are the merciful' (Matthew 5:7) (1).
   - Catholics believe that kindness and compassion are key teachings in their religion (1). They believe they will be judged after death by God on whether they have behaved and acted in a kind and compassionate way towards others, including criminals (1).

   Other valid answers will be accepted.

39 Treatment of criminals

1. "Criminals should have human rights." Be sure to make your points specific, and refer to teachings and views, as you are instructed. You can support your arguments with biblical or other teachings. Make sure you give balanced views and then draw a conclusion – make sure you say why this is your conclusion. (12)

   Arguments for the statement:
   - Catholics would agree with the statement. They believe that all life is sacred because it is God's creation and the Bible teaches that people are of equal value, for example by saying 'you are all one in Christ Jesus' (Galatians 3:28). Christians believe that while criminals deserve punishment, they should still have human rights in order to follow these teachings.
   - Catholics believe that criminals should have human rights such as the right to a fair trial. Bible teachings support this, for example: 'Does our law condemn a man without first hearing him to find out what he has been doing?' (John 7:51). This teaching shows the importance of justice when a person is accused of a crime, including the right to a fair hearing.
   - The Catholic Church teaches that it is important to help those who have done wrong through social teaching, demonstrating that criminals should be given some human rights. Catholics may work in their local communities to help with the rehabilitation of criminals or to support the families of those who are imprisoned to ensure they are treated fairly.

   Arguments against the statement:
   - Some people may feel that criminals should not expect fair treatment if they have committed very serious crimes. For example, if they have taken away a person's life, it is difficult for others to accept this and to treat them fairly. For this reason, people may think it is right that criminals do not have human rights.
   - Christianity promotes ideas of justice and punishment through the Bible. When a crime has been committed, some teachings suggest that, to achieve justice, criminals deserve to have some of their human rights taken away – in particular their freedom if it means that society is protected.
   - Ethical theories such as situation ethics support the act of doing 'the most loving thing'. In cases where offenders are causing ongoing suffering for their victims, this may justify a criminal being tortured or not treated fairly in order to end the suffering of their victims, the victims' families and society in general.

   Other valid answers will be accepted.

40 Capital punishment

1. One mark will be awarded for providing each reason and a second mark for development of the reason up to a maximum of four marks. (4)
   - Genesis 9:6 can be used to support the use of the death penalty and some Catholics may follow this teaching (1). It says 'whoever sheds human blood, by humans shall their blood be shed', suggesting that the death penalty is acceptable for those who have taken the lives of others (1).
   - Some Catholics may argue that the Church has used the death penalty and so its use can be justified in certain circumstances (1). In the Middle Ages, the death penalty was used for crimes such as challenging the authority of the Church (1).
   - Catholics may point to the teaching of St Paul in Romans 13, who states that they should obey the laws of the country where they live: 'Let everyone be subject to the governing authorities' (1). If the government of the country uses the death penalty as a punishment for the most serious crimes, this Bible teaching suggests that it is justifiable to support this (1).

   Other valid answers will be accepted.

2. One mark will be awarded for providing each reason and a second mark for development of the reason up to a maximum of four marks. One further mark will be awarded for any relevant source of wisdom and authority. (5)
   - Jesus taught that revenge was wrong and that people should work to forgive each other (1). He even forgave those who put him to death (1): 'Father, forgive them, for they do not know what they are doing.' (Luke 23:34) (1)
   - The sanctity of life argument states that all life is special (1). As Catholics believe that human life is created by God, many think it is wrong to end life in any way, including by the death penalty (1): 'You shall not murder.' (Exodus 20:13) (1)
   - The Catholic Church Catechism states that the death penalty is wrong and is not supported by the Church (1). Many popes have spoken out against the use of the death penalty (1): 'God alone is the Lord of life from its beginning until its end: no one can under any circumstance claim for himself the right directly to destroy an innocent human being.' (CCC 2258) (1)

   Other valid answers will be accepted.

UNIT 6: PEACE AND CONFLICT

41 Peace

1. One mark will be awarded for each point identified up to a maximum of three marks. (3)
   - Jesus is called the 'Prince of Peace' (1).
   - Jesus told his disciples not to fight (Luke 22:49–51) (1).
   - Jesus showed that people should live in peace with each other (1).

- Jesus taught 'Blessed are the peacemakers' (Matthew 5:9) (1).
- Jesus taught 'Love your neighbour as yourself' (Mark 12:31) (1).

Other valid answers will be accepted.

2 One mark will be awarded for providing each reason and a second mark for development of the reason up to a maximum of four marks. (4)
- Catholics follow the example of Jesus, who gave many teachings about peace (1). For example, in the Sermon on the Mount he taught 'Blessed are the peacemakers' (Matthew 5:9) (1).
- The importance of seeking peace and justice are key teachings of the Catholic Church Catechism (1). It is believed that this is how God intended humans to live together in the world (1).
- Catholics believe that all Church members are united through peace (1). The sign of peace (a handshake) is an important feature of Mass (1).

Other valid answers will be accepted.

42 Peacemaking

1 One mark will be awarded for providing each reason and a second mark for development of the reason up to a maximum of four marks. One further mark will be awarded for any relevant source of wisdom and authority. (5)
- Catholics work for peace because they believe that this is a duty given to them by God (1). They believe that one way of helping others is to work for peace in areas of the world where there is conflict (1): 'Be kind and compassionate to one another.' (Ephesians 4:32) (1)
- Catholics follow the example of Jesus, who worked for and taught about the importance of peace (1). They believe that this is how God intended the world to be (1): 'Blessed are the peacemakers.' (Matthew 5:9) (1)
- The Catholic Church Catechism teaches that peace, reconciliation and forgiveness are the ways to resolve conflict in the world (1). Organisations such as Pax Christi encourage people to resolve their conflicts through peace and reconciliation, thereby putting Catholic teachings into action (1): 'Peace is the work of justice and the effect of charity.' (CCC 2304) (1)

Other valid answers will be accepted.

2 One mark will be awarded for providing each way and a second mark for development of the way up to a maximum of four marks. (4)
- Catholics can work with movements like Pax Christi, a Catholic organisation that works for peace and justice (1). They work with governments to find peaceful ways of resolving conflict (1).
- Catholics can work to educate others about the importance of peace (1). They can go into schools and share messages of peace, and show people how to overcome conflict through their teachings (1).
- Catholics can take part in public demonstrations to promote peace (1). They can oppose conflict and violence in the world, and try to put their teachings of peace into practice (1).

Other valid answers will be accepted.

43 Conflict

1 "Religion can bring peace." Be sure to make your points specific, and refer to teachings and views, as you are instructed. You can support your arguments with biblical or other teachings. Make sure you give balanced views and then draw a conclusion – make sure you say why this is your conclusion. (12)

Arguments for the statement:
- Catholics believe that their religion teaches peace. The Bible contains teachings such as 'in me you may have peace' (John 16:33), which supports the idea that God intended people to live peacefully together in the world.
- Catholics follow the example of Jesus, who taught about the importance of peace. 'Blessed are the peacemakers' (Matthew 5:9) and 'all who draw the sword will die by the sword' (Matthew 26:52) are key teachings for peace and against violence. Catholics believe they should try to follow these teachings to bring about peace in the world.
- Catholic organisations such as Pax Christi work to achieve peace in the world by putting Catholic teachings into action. They believe that through methods such as discussion and reconciliation they can work to reduce conflict in countries around the world and to educate people about the importance of world peace.

Arguments against the statement:
- Some non-religious people may believe that religion cannot bring peace. They may even believe that religion is sometimes at the root of conflict, as seen, for example, in recent acts of terrorism by religious extremists. They may think that differences in religious practices are the cause of wars rather than the source of solutions to end conflict.
- Humanists may claim that religion contributes to conflict in the world as it divides people on their beliefs. They may argue that religions work against each other and cause tension between people rather than reducing it.
- Some Catholics may believe that religion can help work to bring peace, but that ultimately it is those in authority, such as governments, who hold the real power to bring peace and that there is little that ordinary individuals can do.

Other valid answers will be accepted.

44 Pacifism

1 One mark will be awarded for each point identified up to a maximum of three marks. (3)
- One Catholic teaching is 'You shall not murder' (Exodus 20:13) (1).
- Being pacifist means to 'Love your neighbour as yourself' (Mark 12:31) (1).
- Jesus taught that it is important to 'love your enemies and pray for those who persecute you' (Matthew 5:43–44) (1).
- Jesus wouldn't allow his disciples to use violence, saying 'Put your sword back in its place' (Matthew 26:52) (1).
- The Catholic Church teaches that all life is sacred as humans are made 'in the image of God' (Genesis 1:27) (1).

Other valid answers will be accepted.

2 One mark will be awarded for providing each reason and a second mark for development of the reason up to a maximum of four marks. (4)
- There are many Bible teachings from Jesus concerning ideas of peace (1). For example, he taught 'You have heard that it was said, "Love your neighbour and hate your enemy." But I tell you, love your enemies and pray for those who persecute you.' (Matthew 5:43–44) (1)
- The Bible contains many teachings that seem to support pacifism (1), for example 'Put your sword back in its place … for all who draw the sword will die by the sword.' (Matthew 26:52) (1)
- Life is seen as sacred because it is God's creation (1). Any use of violence threatens life, which goes against teachings such as the Ten Commandments (1).

Other valid answers will be accepted.

45 The Just War theory

1 One mark will be awarded for each point identified up to a maximum of three marks. (3)
- A Just War theory condition is that war must be fought for a just cause (1).
- A Just War theory condition is that war must be declared by a proper authority (1).
- A Just War theory condition is that war must be fought to restore peace (1).
- A Just War theory condition is that war must be a last resort (1).
- A Just War theory condition is that innocent civilians must never be the target (1).

Other valid answers will be accepted.

2 One mark will be awarded for providing each reason and a second mark for development of the reason up to a maximum of four marks. (4)
   - Catholics may think that war can be justified if the conditions of the Just War Doctrine in the Catholic Catechism are met (1). For example, war can only be fought as a last resort and if all other avenues to peace have been exhausted (1).
   - Catholics may believe that while peace is important, there are circumstances in which war is 'the lesser of two evils' (1). For example, war may be justified to protect the innocent in society (1).
   - Jesus and St Paul taught that obedience should be shown to the government of a country, which could command war (1). This means some Catholics may believe that if a country decides to go to war, the people in the country should support it, as the authorities have been put in place by God and so it is God's will (1).
   Other valid answers will be accepted.

46 Holy war
1 "Holy war is always wrong." Be sure to make your points specific, and refer to teachings and views, as you are instructed. You can support your arguments with biblical or other teachings. Make sure you give balanced views and then draw a conclusion – make sure you say why this is your conclusion. (12)
   Arguments for the statement:
   - Catholics support ideas of peace first and foremost. There are many Bible teachings on the importance of peace such as 'Blessed are the peacemakers, for they will be called children of God.' (Matthew 5:9)
   - Many of Jesus' teachings support the view that war is never the answer. He encouraged love and compassion towards enemies through teachings such as 'love your enemies and pray for those who persecute you.' (Matthew 5:44)
   - Many non-religious people may believe that religion itself is a cause of war and therefore never the right action. Although not for religious reasons, they may also value human life and believe that peaceful methods should be found to resolve conflict.
   Arguments against the statement:
   - Catholics may sometimes feel that war is necessary if it is in defence of their religion – they have historically fought in wars of religious conflict such as the Thirty Years War.
   - There is some biblical and Church support for war as an act of self-defence against an aggressor. The Catholic Catechism teaches: 'However, "as long as the danger of war persists and there is no international authority with the necessary competence and power, governments cannot be denied the right of lawful self-defence, once all peace efforts have failed".' (CCC 2308)
   - Non-religious people may oppose war in general on the grounds of religion, but they may recognise that modern-day threats such as terrorism require a counterattack in order to bring about peace. They may feel that there is no alternative to force once all peaceful methods have been tried and have failed.
   Other valid answers will be accepted.

47 Weapons of mass destruction
1 One mark will be awarded for each point identified up to a maximum of three marks. (3)
   - Catholics believe that weapons of mass destruction (WMD) cause too much damage to God's creation (1).
   - Catholics believe that WMD threaten and harm innocent lives (1).
   - Catholics believe that WMD do not respect the sanctity of human life (1).
   - Catholics believe that the use of WMD cannot be justified (1).
   - Catholics believe that the conditions of Just War theory cannot be met through the use of WMD (1).
   Other valid answers will be accepted.
2 One mark will be awarded for providing each reason and a second mark for development of the reason up to a maximum of four marks. (4)
   - WMD do not distinguish between soldiers and innocent people (1). They cause as much destruction as possible (1).
   - WMD do not respect the sanctity of human life (1). Catholics believe that human life is sacred as it is created by God and should be preserved (1).
   - WMD cause widespread damage to the environment (1). As God created the world, it should be respected and cared for, not destroyed (1).
   Other valid answers will be accepted.

48 Issues surrounding conflict
1 One mark will be awarded for providing each reason and a second mark for development of the reason up to a maximum of four marks. One further mark will be awarded for any relevant source of wisdom and authority. (5)
   - Catholics teach about the importance of peace (1). Teachings from the Catholic Church Catechism such as 'Terrorism threatens, wounds, and kills indiscriminately; it is gravely against justice and charity' (CCC 2297) (1) show that terrorism is wrong (1).
   - Catholics follow the example of Jesus, who showed that justice and peace are important (1). He gave teachings that Catholics try to follow in their own lives in order to be rewarded in heaven with God (1): 'Blessed are the peacemakers.' (Matthew 5:9) (1)
   - Catholics do not advocate the use of violence, even in retaliation (1). They believe that peaceful methods should be found to resolve conflict, not violent means such as terrorism (1): 'But to you who are listening I say: love your enemies, do good to those who hate you, bless those who curse you, pray for those who ill-treat you. If someone slaps you on one cheek, turn to them the other also. If someone takes your coat, do not withhold your shirt from them. Give to everyone who asks you, and if anyone takes what belongs to you, do not demand it back. Do to others as you would have them do to you.' (Luke 6:27–31) (1)
   Other valid answers will be accepted.
2 One mark will be awarded for providing each way and a second mark for development of the way up to a maximum of four marks. (4)
   - Dorothy Day was a Catholic who campaigned against social injustice and conflict in the world (1). She founded the newspaper *Catholic Worker* to challenge examples of injustice (1).
   - The Catholic priest Oscar Romero stood up against violence and oppression (1). He spoke out against the injustices in his community, working with those living in poverty to try to help to overcome their suffering (1).
   - Individual Catholics can put the teachings given to them in the Bible and by the Church into action (1). They can offer practical help to those who need it, believing that God gave them this duty (1).
   Other valid answers will be accepted.

UNIT 7: PHILOSOPHY OF RELIGION
49 Revelation
1 One mark will be awarded for each point identified up to a maximum of three marks. (3)
   - The revelation of Jesus shows that God is omnipotent (1).
   - The revelation of Jesus shows that God is benevolent (1).
   - The revelation of Jesus as the Son of God shows that God the Father is part of the Trinity (1).
   - The revelation of Jesus shows that God is immanent (1).
   - The revelation of Jesus shows that God is transcendent (1).
   Other valid answers will be accepted.

2 One mark will be awarded for providing each reason and a second mark for development of the reason up to a maximum of four marks. (4)
- Jesus is believed to be the Son of God and is the second part of the Trinity (1). He is God incarnate – God in human form – who helps Catholics to 'know' God better (1).
- Jesus is the culmination of God's revelation (1). Catholics believe that he came to the world to save humankind from the sins of humanity, so is of the utmost importance (1).
- For Catholics, Jesus is a prophet sent by God for a specific purpose (1). He confirms their belief in the afterlife and strengthens their faith (1).

Other valid answers will be accepted.

50 Visions (1)
1 One mark will be awarded for each point identified up to a maximum of three marks. (3)
- Catholics accept the vision of the Virgin Mary received by St Bernadette (1).
- Catholics believe Abraham had a vision of a burning bush (1).
- Catholics believe that Jesus received visions in the Bible (1).
- A person who had a vision was Joan of Arc (1).
- Catholics believe that St Paul/Saul received a vision on the road to Damascus (1).

Other valid answers will be accepted.

2 One mark will be awarded for providing each reason and a second mark for development of the reason up to a maximum of four marks. (4)
- Visions show how God wants to communicate with humanity (1). Examples such as Abraham show that God wanted to pass on important messages about his benevolence (1).
- There have been many famous Catholics who have received vision-type experiences of God (1). For example, Bernadette's vision of the Virgin Mary is important to Catholics (1).
- Visions help to strengthen Catholics' faith (1). They are physically witnessed, which reinforces and confirms their belief in God (1).

Other valid answers will be accepted.

51 Visions (2)
1 "Visions are good evidence of God's existence." Be sure to make your points specific, and refer to teachings and views, as you are instructed. You can support your arguments with biblical or other teachings. Make sure you give balanced views and then draw a conclusion – make sure you say why this is your conclusion. (12)

Arguments for the statement:
- Catholics believe that visions are a method God uses to directly contact humans, and so are good evidence of his existence. Visions such as the transfiguration of Jesus allow God to reveal Jesus as the connection between humanity and the Divine.
- Catholics believe that God's nature can be revealed through visions. The example of Abraham's vision of God allowed God to be revealed as caring and benevolent, proving not only his existence but also what he is like.
- Catholics believe that visions may be a good way of allowing humans to develop a relationship with God. In the example of Joan of Arc, her visions allowed her to understand God better and influenced her conduct.

Arguments against the statement:
- Some Catholics accept that visions occur but do not place as much importance on them as other forms of revelation. They may accept that the Bible or the example of Jesus are better forms of revelation in revealing both the nature and the existence of God.
- Non-religious people may argue that visions are not 'proof' of God's existence as they are simply hallucinations that are misunderstood. They may argue that only things which can be verified scientifically should be accepted and that the existence of God cannot, therefore, be proved through visions.
- Non-religious people may claim that visions are not real and therefore cannot be trusted. They may believe that they are simply hoaxes or illusions and therefore not proof of God's existence.

Other valid answers will be accepted.

52 Miracles
1 "Miracles are proof of God's existence." Be sure to make your points specific, and refer to teachings and views, as you are instructed. You can support your arguments with biblical or other teachings. Make sure you give balanced views and then draw a conclusion – make sure you say why this is your conclusion. (12)

Arguments for the statement:
- Catholics believe that miracles demonstrate the nature of God and, through this, his existence. Miracles such as those received by St Bernadette show God's power and his care for his creation, and thus are proof of his existence.
- Catholics believe that miracles can strengthen the faith of believers. They provide comfort that God is close and active in the world.
- Catholics may believe that miracles cannot be explained any other way than through God. Science cannot offer a satisfactory explanation and they are therefore proof that God exists and is present in the world.

Arguments against the statement:
- Some Catholics accept that miracles demonstrate the characteristics of God, such as his omnipotence and benevolence, but place less emphasis on them, believing that God can be revealed in other ways, such as the Bible. They may believe that having faith means putting their trust in God, meaning that he does not need to reveal himself through miracles in order for them to accept that he is real.
- Non-religious people may argue that there are scientific explanations for miracles and that they, therefore, do not 'prove' the existence of God or reveal what he might be like. They claim that science can offer rational and measurable theories for miracles that do not involve God.
- Non-religious people may point to the uncertainty surrounding miracles. As people can experience and interpret them differently, they are not reliable proof of God's existence. This may also lead them to question why God would leave people in such uncertainty if he does actually exist.

Other valid answers will be accepted.

53 Religious experiences
1 One mark will be awarded for each point identified up to a maximum of three marks. (3)
- Religious experiences help to confirm Catholic belief in God (1).
- The Catholic Church does not approve all religious experiences (1).
- Catholics believe that religious experiences can help them to know God better (1).
- Some Catholics may consider religious experiences to be subjective and open to interpretation (1).
- Some Catholics may believe that they do not need religious experiences to prove that God exists (1).

Other valid answers will be accepted.

2 One mark will be awarded for providing each way and a second mark for development of the way up to a maximum of four marks. (4)
- Catholics may respond by arguing that there are many examples of religious experiences that have been verified and accepted by the Catholic Church (1), and so they are real and valid (1).

- Catholics might respond by saying that religious believers have no reason to lie about religious experiences (1). Religious believers have faith in God and do not need to prove it to themselves or to others (1).
- Catholics could respond by claiming that the nature of God is revealed through religious experiences, which confirms his existence (1). For example, miracles such as those received by St Bernadette show God's power and his love for his creation (1).

Other valid answers will be accepted.

54 The design argument

1 "The design argument proves there is a God." Be sure to make your points specific, and refer to teachings and views, as you are instructed. You can support your arguments with biblical or other teachings. Make sure you give balanced views and then draw a conclusion – make sure you say why this is your conclusion. (12)

Arguments for the statement:
- The design argument offers an explanation for the evidence of design in the world that can be seen in nature. As William Paley illustrated, the fact that so many things in the world appear to be designed for their individual purpose suggests that there is a designer behind it, which, Catholics believe, has to be God. This is in line with Catholic teachings and confirms Catholic faith.
- Catholics support the design argument because they can use it to respond to criticisms such as evolution being the explanation for design in the world, not God. Catholics argue that evolution is the tool used by God to create humans, so religion and science are not in conflict.
- Catholics agree with the design argument as they believe that the creation of the world is evidence of God's purpose and of his nature. God is shown to be all-powerful, benevolent and, at the same time, beyond human understanding in his planning and design of the universe.

Arguments against the statement:
- People with non-religious views may say that God is not needed to explain the design in the world as the scientific theory of evolution provides the full explanation. This discredits the design argument and also the argument that God exists.
- There is evidence of bad design in the world, such as earthquakes and volcanoes. Non-religious people could use this to argue either that God does not exist, or that if he does exist, he is not the omnipotent and benevolent God Catholics claim him to be. They may ask why God designed things that cause human suffering and use this fact to deny his existence.
- Some Catholics may argue that while they believe God designed the universe, they do not feel that the design argument provides good proof of his existence. They may believe that Catholic sources of authority such as the Bible or traditional Catholic teachings such as the Catechism provide better evidence of God's existence.

Other valid answers will be accepted.

55 The cosmological argument

1 One mark will be awarded for each point identified up to a maximum of three marks. (3)
- The cosmological argument shows that God is the creator of the universe (1).
- The cosmological argument shows that God is omnipotent (1).
- The cosmological argument shows that God is benevolent (1).
- The cosmological argument shows that God is unknowable (1).
- The cosmological argument shows that God is omniscient (1).

Other valid answers will be accepted.

2 One mark will be awarded for providing each reason and a second mark for development of the reason up to a maximum of four marks. (4)
- Catholics use the cosmological argument to prove that as the universe exists, God must exist as its first cause (1). Catholics believe that there must be a reason for how and why the universe came to exist, and the cosmological argument confirms their faith that it must have been God who caused it to happen (1).
- Catholics can use the cosmological argument to respond to scientific criticisms that the 'Big Bang' alone caused the world to come into existence (1). Catholics argue that God caused the 'Big Bang', which led to the creation of the world, demonstrating that science and religion can work together (1).
- Catholics claim that the cosmological argument is in line with Bible teachings (1). Genesis states that God created the universe and the cosmological argument can be used to support this teaching (1).

Other valid answers will be accepted.

56 The existence of suffering

1 One mark will be awarded for providing each reason and a second mark for development of the reason up to a maximum of four marks. (4)
- Suffering may make Catholics question the nature of God (1). They may ask whether God can be omnipotent if he does not have the power to prevent suffering (1).
- The problem of suffering causes some Catholics to question whether God loves his creation (1). They may ask why, if he loved his creation and was benevolent, he doesn't care enough to stop the suffering in the world (1).
- The problem of suffering causes some Catholics to question the very existence of God (1). The continued presence of suffering in the world could call into question the existence of an all-knowing God (1).

Other valid answers will be accepted.

2 One mark will be awarded for providing each reason and a second mark for development of the reason up to a maximum of four marks. (4)
- Suffering could challenge a Catholic person's religious faith (1). They may look at the amount of suffering in the world and question whether God actually exists (1).
- Suffering could cause Catholics to question the characteristics that they believe God has (1). They may question whether God is omnipotent, omniscient and benevolent if he doesn't do anything to stop evil and suffering in the world (1).
- Suffering could help to strengthen a Catholic person's faith (1). It may lead them to accept the transcendent nature of God, in that they do not understand every aspect of what God is like (1).

Other valid answers will be accepted.

57 Solutions to the problem of suffering

1 One mark will be awarded for providing each reason and a second mark for development of the reason up to a maximum of four marks. One further mark will be awarded for any relevant source of wisdom and authority. (5)
- Catholics believe that suffering could be seen as a test of faith (1). This can be seen in the Bible through the example of Job, who suffered but never doubted the existence of God (1): 'In all this, Job did not sin by charging God with wrongdoing.' (Job 1:22) (1)
- Catholics believe that the book of Psalms shows them what the purpose of suffering is (1). It allows them the opportunity to follow the example of Jesus in order to live as God intended (1): 'Let me live that I may praise you, and may your laws sustain me. I have strayed like a lost sheep. Seek your servant, for I have not forgotten your commands.' (Psalm 119:175–176) (1)

- Catholics believe that the purpose of suffering could be to encourage people to help others (1). When people are suffering, prayer or charity work can be used to support them and Catholics believe that God gave them the duty of helping others (1): 'Love your neighbour as yourself.' (Mark 12:31) (1)

Other valid answers will be accepted.

2 One mark will be awarded for providing each way and a second mark for development of the way up to a maximum of four marks. (4)
- Catholics could respond to the problem of suffering through prayer (1). Praying to God can bring hope and comfort for those who are suffering (1).
- Catholics believe that they should follow the example of Job from the Bible (1). He saw suffering as a test of faith and a challenge not to lose his belief in God (1).
- Catholics can respond to the problem of suffering through charity work (1). Giving practical aid or working with a charity such as Christian Aid can help to reduce suffering and support those in need, which Catholics believe is a duty from God (1).

Other valid answers will be accepted.

UNIT 8: EQUALITY

58 Human rights

1 One mark will be awarded for providing each reason and a second mark for development of the reason up to a maximum of four marks. (4)
- Catholics believe that all humans are created by God and so deserve to have human rights (1). They believe that humans are special as they are made 'in the image of God' (Genesis 1:27) and should all receive equal and fair treatment (1).
- Justice is important to Catholics and human rights support this (1). Jesus gave many teachings such as 'treat others as you would like to be treated' that support ideas of justice (1).
- Catholics believe that the Bible contains many teachings that support human rights (1). For example, the Ten Commandments teach Catholics how they should behave (1).

Other valid answers will be accepted.

2 One mark will be awarded for providing each reason and a second mark for development of the reason up to a maximum of four marks. One further mark will be awarded for any relevant source of wisdom and authority. (5)
- Catholics believe that there are many teachings in the Bible that uphold the idea of human rights (1). For example, the Ten Commandments teach Catholics to uphold the right to life (1): 'You shall not murder.' (Exodus 20:13) (1)
- Catholics believe that all humans deserve fair and just treatment because God himself is just (1). Jesus treated all people as having equal rights, including those of lower social status such as women and lepers (1): 'So in Christ Jesus you are all children of God through faith, for all of you who were baptised into Christ have clothed yourselves with Christ.' (Galatians 3:26–27) (1)
- The Bible teaches that all humans are made 'in the image of God' (1). They are made to be equal so should all have the same human rights (1): 'So God created mankind in his own image, in the image of God he created them; male and female he created them.' (Genesis 1:27) (1)

Other valid answers will be accepted.

59 Equality

1 "Religion can help to achieve equality." Be sure to make your points specific, and refer to teachings and views, as you are instructed. You can support your arguments with biblical or other teachings. Make sure you give balanced views and then draw a conclusion – make sure you say why this is your conclusion. (12)

Arguments for the statement:
- The Catholic Church has many teachings about equality. The Bible teaches that God created humans 'in his own image' (Genesis 1:27), thereby making them special and of equal worth. Catholics try to put these teachings into practice to achieve equality for all.
- Jesus demonstrated ideas of equality and justice in his treatment of others. In teachings such as 'Love your neighbour as yourself' (Mark 12:31) and 'do to others as you would have them do to you' (Luke 6:31), Jesus promoted ideas of fair and equal treatment for all.
- There are many Catholics working for equality in the world, putting Catholic teachings into practice. Mother Teresa worked to bring equality to those living in poverty, and the current pope raises awareness of issues of inequality around the world.

Arguments against the statement:
- Some Catholics may believe that religion can help to provide messages of equality, but that if people do not put them into action, equality will not be achieved.
- There are examples of inequality within Catholicism. On the one hand, men and women are viewed as being equal as this is how God created them; on the other hand, they are viewed as being suited to different roles, resulting in possible inequality – for example, only men can become Catholic priests.
- Some Catholics may believe that religion is not a cause of inequality and therefore does not have a responsibility to fight it. They may believe that only official authorities and governments have the power to overcome social injustice and inequality.

Other valid answers will be accepted.

60 Religious freedom

1 One mark will be awarded for each point identified up to a maximum of three marks. (3)
- One benefit of a multifaith society is greater religious tolerance (1).
- One benefit of a multifaith society is the ability to experience other religious traditions (1).
- One benefit of a multifaith society is better understanding and communication among people of all religions (1).
- One benefit of a multifaith society is unity through groups working together for common goals (1).
- One benefit of a multifaith society is less discrimination and poor treatment of people from minority faiths (1).

Other valid answers will be accepted.

2 One mark will be awarded for each point identified up to a maximum of three marks. (3)
- One challenge of living in a multifaith society is that groups may face discrimination because of their religion (1).
- One challenge of living in a multifaith society is an increase in religious hatred and the persecution of people from different religions (1).
- One challenge of living in a multifaith society is an increase in religious tension between different religious groups (1).
- One challenge of living in a multifaith society is that some minority group views may be ignored (1).
- One challenge of living in a multifaith society is a lack of communication between different faiths (1).

Other valid answers will be accepted.

61 Religious prejudice and discrimination

1 One mark will be awarded for providing each attitude and a second mark for development of the attitude up to a maximum of four marks. One further mark will be awarded for any relevant source of wisdom and authority. (5)
- Catholics teach about agape love, which should be shown towards all humans and therefore towards all religions (1). This is unconditional love as taught by Jesus (1): 'A new command I give you: love one another. As I have loved you, so you must love one another.' (John 13:34) (1)

- The Catholic Church teaches that all religions should be free to practise their faith as all people deserve dignity (1). The Catechism teaches that religious freedom is an 'inalienable' right (1): 'The right to the exercise of freedom, especially in moral and religious matters, is an inalienable requirement of the dignity of the human person.' (CCC 1738) (1)
- Some Catholics may feel threatened by the growth of other religions and claim that Catholicism is the only true faith (1). They may feel that their religion is being threatened and cling more tightly to their traditions and practices (1).

Other valid answers will be accepted.

62 Racial harmony

1. One mark will be awarded for each point identified up to a maximum of three marks. (3)
    - The Catholic Church teaches that all humans are made 'in the image of God' (Genesis 1:27) (1).
    - St Paul taught that all people are from one nation (1).
    - Catholics believe that they have a duty to help others regardless of their race (1).
    - Jesus taught people to love each other regardless of their race (1).
    - Bible teachings support the idea of racial harmony within society (1).

    Other valid answers will be accepted.

2. One mark will be awarded for providing each way and a second mark for development of the way up to a maximum of four marks. (3)
    - Individual Catholic Church leaders are from many ethnic backgrounds and promote racial harmony (1). They have worked nationally and internationally to promote unity between all races (1).
    - The Catholic Church encourages equality, tolerance and respect (1). They use key Catholic teachings, including those referring to 'the equal dignity of human persons' (CCC 1947) (1).
    - Catholic organisations, such as the Catholic Association for Racial Justice (CARJ), work for unity between different races (1). They develop community cohesion and try to remove barriers between people of different races (1).

    Other valid answers will be accepted.

63 Racial discrimination

1. One mark will be awarded for each point identified up to a maximum of three marks. (3)
    - Racial discrimination can cause a lack of respect in society (1).
    - Racial discrimination can cause bad feeling between different races (1).
    - Racial discrimination can cause a lack of trust between groups (1).
    - Racial discrimination can have a negative impact on people's wellbeing (1).
    - Racial discrimination can result in a lack of access to resources (1).

    Other valid answers will be accepted.

2. One mark will be awarded for providing each reason and a second mark for development of the reason up to a maximum of four marks. (4)
    - Catholics believe that God sees no difference between people from different races (1). The Bible teaches 'for you are all one in Christ Jesus' (Galatians 3:28) (1).
    - Jesus condemned the unfair treatment of people based on their ethnic background (1). His teaching in the Parable of the Good Samaritan demonstrates ideas of compassion towards everyone (1).
    - The Bible teaches 'from one man he made all the nations, that they should inhabit the whole earth' (Acts 17:26) (1). It supports the view that God does not show favouritism towards any one race (1).

    Other valid answers will be accepted.

64 Social justice

1. One mark will be awarded for each point identified up to a maximum of three marks. (3)
    - Catholics can organise food banks in their local communities to help those in need (1).
    - Catholics can promote ideas of social justice in their communities (1).
    - Catholic leaders educate others about social justice (1).
    - Catholics can get involved in charity work to fight the social injustice of poverty (1).
    - Catholic organisations such as CAFOD tackle issues of social injustice globally (1).

    Other valid answers will be accepted.

2. One mark will be awarded for providing each reason and a second mark for development of the reason up to a maximum of four marks. (4)
    - Catholics believe that they have a duty from God to work for social justice (1). Stewardship means to care for God's creation, which includes other humans (1).
    - The Catholic Church and the pope both teach the importance of social justice (1): 'The duty of making oneself a neighbour to others and actively serving them becomes even more urgent when it involves the disadvantaged, in whatever area this may be.' (CCC 1932)
    - Catholics refer to Bible teachings promoting the idea of helping others, including those who are less fortunate (1). Jesus taught 'whatever you did for one of the least of these brothers and sisters of mine, you did for me' (Matthew 25:40) (1).

    Other valid answers will be accepted.

65 Wealth and poverty

1. "Inequality is the cause of all social injustice in the world." Be sure to make your points specific, and refer to teachings and views, as you are instructed. You can support your arguments with biblical or other teachings. Make sure you give balanced views and then draw a conclusion – make sure you say why this is your conclusion. (12)

    Arguments for the statement:
    - Some Catholics believe that inequality is one of the main causes of social injustice.
    - Catholics believe that they should follow the example of Jesus, who taught that people have a responsibility to care for others, including those less fortunate than themselves. Jesus taught, for example, that wealth should be shared and that compassion be shown to others.
    - Catholics may feel that inequality is at the root of all social problems as it can result in a lack of communication between groups, as well as prejudice and discrimination.

    Arguments against the statement:
    - Catholics may believe that inequality is one cause of social injustice, but that there are many others of equal importance, including population growth and unstable political situations.
    - Some Catholics may believe that inequality is the result of people not living their lives as God intended. They may think that if people lived their lives according to Catholic principles, there would be less social injustice.
    - Some Catholics may believe that the only way to solve social injustice is through religion. They may believe that turning to God and asking for help will improve the world situation.

    Other valid answers will be accepted.

Islam

UNIT 1: MUSLIM BELIEFS

66 The Six Beliefs of Islam

1. One mark will be awarded for each point identified up to a maximum of three marks. (3)
    - One feature of the Six Beliefs of Sunni Islam is belief in one God (1).

- One feature of the Six Beliefs is belief in angels (1).
- One feature of the Six Beliefs is the authority of holy books (1).
- One feature of the Six Beliefs is prophethood (1).
- One feature of the Six Beliefs is the belief in predestination (1).
- One feature of the Six Beliefs is belief in life after death (1).

Other valid answers will be accepted.

2 One mark will be awarded for providing each reason and a second mark for development of the reason up to a maximum of four marks. (4)
- The Six Beliefs help all Sunni Muslims to better understand their religion, Islam. For example, they all accept the belief that there is one God called Allah (1).
- They show Sunni Muslims how to live their lives (1) according to Allah's rules. For example, one of the Six Beliefs is the belief in life after death, which affects how Muslims behave and and how they treat others so that they will be rewarded in the afterlife (1).
- They are the basic principles of Islam accepted by all Sunni Muslims (1). For example, all Sunni Muslims recognise the importance of prophethood as God's way of communicating with humanity (1).

Other valid answers will be accepted.

67 The five roots of 'Usul ad-Din in Shi'a Islam

1 One mark will be awarded for providing each reason and a second mark for development of the reason up to a maximum of four marks. (4)
- The five roots of 'Usul ad-Din are all based on the concept of Tawhid (the oneness of Allah) (1). For example, everything a Muslim does is linked to the concept of submitting to Allah in all aspects of their life (1).
- Tawhid is important because Muslim prayers are directed five times a day to Allah (1). Regular communication addressed to Allah through prayer helps Muslims to understand him better (1).
- Tawhid is a central idea in Islam and is given prominence in the Qur'an through Surah 112 (1). This refers to Allah as: 'The Self-Sufficient Master, Whom all creatures need.' (Surah 112:2) (1)

Other valid answers will be accepted.

2 One mark will be awarded for providing each root and a second mark for development of the root up to a maximum of four marks. (4)
- One of the five roots of 'Usul ad-Din is Tawhid (1), the oneness of God called Allah (1).
- One of the five roots of 'Usul ad-Din is Adl (1). Muslims believe Allah is fair and just in his treatment of everything (1).
- One of the five roots of 'Usul ad-Din is Nubuwwah (1). This is the belief in prophets appointed by Allah to pass on messages to humanity (1).

Other valid answers will be accepted.

68 The nature of Allah

1 One mark will be awarded for each point identified up to a maximum of three marks. (3)
- Muslims believe Allah is transcendent (1).
- Muslims believe Allah is merciful (1).
- Muslims believe Allah is immanent (1).
- Muslims believe Allah will judge humans after death (1).
- Muslims believe Allah is loving (1).

Other valid answers will be accepted.

2 One mark will be awarded for providing each way and a second mark for development of the way up to a maximum of four marks. One further mark will be awarded for any relevant source of wisdom and authority. (5)
- Allah is described in the Qur'an as being transcendent, beyond human understanding (1). Muslims use his 99 names to help them understand what he is like (1): 'And the Most Beautiful Names belong to Allah, so call on Him by them.' (Surah 7:180) (1)
- Allah is described using the term Tawhid (1), meaning that he is the one God and Muslims should worship only him (1): 'Worship Allah, and avoid Taghut.' (Surah 16:36) (1)
- Allah is described as merciful (1). Muslims believe Allah will forgive them after death if they are sorry for what they have done wrong (1): 'verily Allah forgives all sins. Truly, He is Oft-Forgiving, Most Merciful.' (Surah 39:53) (1)

Other valid answers will be accepted.

69 Risalah

1 One mark will be awarded for each point identified up to a maximum of three marks. (3)
- Prophets are important in Islam as they are messengers of Allah (1).
- Prophets are important as they allow Allah to communicate with humans (1).
- Some prophets are important because they have brought written messages (1).
- Prophets are important as they have shown humans how Allah wants them to live (1).
- Some prophets are important because they have brought warnings from Allah (1).

Other valid answers will be accepted.

2 One mark will be awarded for providing each reason and a second mark for development of the reason up to a maximum of four marks. (4)
- Prophets are important in Islam as Allah uses them to communicate with humanity (1). For example, Ibrahim carried messages from Allah to encourage people to worship God (1).
- Some prophets are important as they have brought holy books from Allah (1), for example Muhammad brought the Qur'an (1).
- Prophets act as examples of how Allah wants Muslims to live their lives (1). Isma'il showed the characteristics of patience and compassion that Muslims should try to develop (1).

Other valid answers will be accepted.

70 Muslim holy books

1 One mark will be awarded for each point identified up to a maximum of three marks. (3)
- The Qur'an was revealed to Muhammad (1).
- It was revealed over 23 years (1).
- The Qur'an is divided into chapters and verses (1).
- Muslims believe the Qur'an came from Allah (1).
- The Qur'an is written in Arabic (1).

Other valid answers will be accepted.

2 One mark will be awarded for providing each reason and a second mark for development of the reason up to a maximum of four marks. (4)
- The Qur'an is important because it is believed to have come directly from Allah (1). Allah revealed it through the angel Jibril (1).
- The Qur'an is used by Muslims in prayer and worship (1). The Imam recites passages from the Qur'an during worship in the mosque (1).
- Muslims believe the Qur'an is a form of revelation of Allah (1). It reveals to Muslims that Allah is all-powerful and loving (1).

Other valid answers will be accepted.

71 Malaikah

1 "Belief in angels is the most important belief in Islam." Be sure to make your points specific, and refer to teachings and views, as you are instructed. You can support your arguments with Qur'anic or other teachings. Make sure you give balanced views and then draw a conclusion – make sure you say why this is your conclusion. In this question, 3 of the marks awarded will be for your spelling, punctuation and grammar, and your use of specialist terminology. (15)

Arguments for the statement:
- A belief in angels is important because Muslims believe Allah uses them to communicate with humans. For example, angels have been used in Islam to pass messages to the prophets, such as when Muhammad received the Qur'an from the angel Jibril.
- Angels in Islam are important as they have significant roles. For example, the Qur'an explains that Izra'il is the angel of death and helps Muslims to understand that they need to live their lives as Allah wishes.
- Important teachings about angels offer proof to Muslims that there is an afterlife. Muslims wish to be rewarded in the afterlife and not punished, so the teaching of Mika'il (the angel of mercy) reassures them that this is possible.

Arguments against the statement:
- Some Muslims accept that a belief in angels is important but do not believe that it is the most important belief in Islam. At the centre of Islam is the belief that Muslims should submit to Allah in all aspects of their lives. This could be considered more important as it underpins all other beliefs.
- Some Muslims would argue that all beliefs in Islam are important and no 'one' belief is more important than another. For example, key Muslim beliefs include belief in the afterlife, belief in Allah and belief in prophethood, which all have equal importance.
- Some Muslims hold that while belief in angels is important, it may be more important to consider how Allah wants them to live their own lives. Putting beliefs into practice may be considered more important as it impacts on their afterlife as well as pleasing Allah.

Other valid answers will be accepted.

72 Al-Qadr
1. One mark will be awarded for each point identified up to a maximum of three marks. (3)
   - Muslims believe that Allah controls everything (1).
   - Al-Qadr is predestination (1).
   - Muslims believe that al-Qadr is linked to the Day of Judgement (1).
   - Al-Qadr is one of the Six Beliefs for Sunni Muslims (1).
   - Shi'a Muslims do not accept al-Qadr (1).

   Other valid answers will be accepted.

2. One mark will be awarded for providing each way and a second mark for development of the way up to a maximum of four marks. (4)
   - Having a belief in al-Qadr (predestination) means that Muslims accept the idea of living their lives according to what Allah wants (1). Muslims want to be rewarded in heaven rather than punished in hell (1).
   - Holding a belief in al-Qadr will make Muslims aware of every action they perform (1). They will want to follow the rules of Allah, for example the Five Pillars (1).
   - A belief in al-Qadr will encourage Muslims to want to help others (1). They believe that behaving in this way, which is commanded in the Qur'an by Allah, will help them to gain favour with him (1).

   Other valid answers will be accepted.

73 Akhirah
1. One mark will be awarded for each point identified up to a maximum of three marks. (3)
   - After death, the angel of death takes a person's soul to barzakh (1).
   - Islam teaches that Muslims will be judged after death by Allah (1).
   - Muslims believe that they can be rewarded in paradise (1).
   - Muslims believe that they can be punished in hell (1).
   - Muslims believe that they will be judged on how they have lived their lives (1).

   Other valid answers will be accepted.

2. One mark will be awarded for providing each way and a second mark for development of the way up to a maximum of four marks. (4)
   - Both Muslims and Christians accept the idea of life being a test for the afterlife (1). They both accept that, after death, humans will be judged by God on how they have lived their lives and behaved towards others (1).
   - Both Muslims and Christians accept the idea of eternal reward or punishment after death (1). They both accept the idea of the reward of heaven or paradise for those who have been good and the punishment of hell for those who have sinned (1).
   - Both Muslims and Christians accept the idea of resurrection (1). They do not believe that death is the end but that the soul and body are reunited in the afterlife (1).

   Other valid answers will be accepted.

UNIT 2: MARRIAGE AND THE FAMILY

74 Marriage
1. One mark will be awarded for each point identified up to a maximum of three marks. (3)
   - Marriage is intended to be for life (1).
   - Marriage is viewed as a legal contract (1).
   - Marriage is between a man and a woman (1).
   - Muslim women are expected to only marry Muslim men (1).
   - Muslim men may marry up to four wives (1).

   Other valid answers will be accepted.

2. One mark will be awarded for providing each reason and a second mark for development of the reason up to a maximum of four marks. (4)
   - Marriage is important to Muslims as it is believed to be the correct context in which to have a family (1). Muslims are expected to get married and to raise their children within the Islamic faith (1).
   - Marriage is a duty commanded by Allah (1). The Qur'an commands: 'marry those among you who are single.' (Surah 24:32) (1)
   - Muslims believe marriage is a stable and strong foundation for society (1). The family unit created within marriage is believed to be a place for the teaching of morals and the difference between right and wrong (1).

   Other valid answers will be accepted.

75 Sexual relationships
1. One mark will be awarded for each point identified up to a maximum of three marks. (3)
   - Muslims believe sex is an act of worship (1).
   - Islam teaches that sexual relationships should only take place within marriage (1).
   - Islam teaches that sexual relationships are intended to fulfil physical, emotional and spiritual needs (1).
   - Islam teaches that sex is a gift from Allah (1).
   - Islam teaches that adultery is always wrong (1).

   Other valid answers will be accepted.

2. One mark will be awarded for providing each reason and a second mark for development of the reason up to a maximum of four marks. One further mark will be awarded for any relevant source of wisdom and authority. (5)
   - Muslims believe that Allah intended sex to take place only within marriage (1). Sex is intended as a gift from Allah for married couples (1): 'When a husband and wife share intimacy it is rewarded, and a blessing from Allah; just as they would be punished if they had engaged in illicit sex.' (Hadith) (1)
   - The Qur'an forbids adultery (1) because sex outside of marriage is seen to break the special relationship between husband and wife (1): 'Nor come nigh to adultery: for it is a shameful deed and an evil, opening the road to other evils.' (Surah 17:32) (1)

- Only sex within marriage is regarded as the correct context in which a husband and wife can satisfy each other's physical, emotional and spiritual needs (1). Islam teaches that this is a duty from Allah and should occur exclusively between a husband and wife (1): 'When a husband and wife share intimacy it is rewarded, and a blessing from Allah.' (Hadith) (1)

Other valid answers will be accepted.

76 Families

1. "The most important purpose of family for Muslims is to strengthen the ummah." Be sure to make your points specific, and refer to teachings and views, as you are instructed. You can support your arguments with Qur'anic or other teachings. Make sure you give balanced views and then draw a conclusion – make sure you say why this is your conclusion. (12)

   Arguments for the statement:
   - Some Muslims agree with the statement as Muslim families often attend the mosque together. This helps to unite all Muslims as they recognise that they are all praying together at the same time each day. Individual family units can feel that they have support and are part of the worldwide ummah through this shared worship.
   - The family unit celebrates important occasions such as Eid and rites of passage such as the birth of a child or the joining of families in marriage. This helps to strengthen the ummah. The local community comes together for these events, demonstrating that there is unity between all Muslims.
   - The ummah has great importance in Islam, with the family being recognised as the first level of the community. The Qur'an teaches that Muslims should be united: 'And hold fast, all of you together, to the Rope of Allah' (Surah 3:103) – a united family unit helps to reinforce and support this teaching.

   Arguments against the statement:
   - Although strengthening the ummah is recognised by Muslims as important, other more practical purposes of the family unit may be considered more important. Another purpose of the family is to care for all of its members; teachings from the Qur'an reinforce the importance of taking care of each other, especially more elderly relatives.
   - Some Muslims may feel that a more important purpose of the family is the education of the young. The family is where children are taught about their faith and the religion of Islam. They are taught how to pray and to follow the rules of Islam; this is an important purpose of the family.
   - Some Muslims may feel that the family is a private unit where people can support, care and love each other. Although the worldwide ummah is recognised as an essential part of Islam, the smaller family unit is where teachings such as respecting and obeying parents are put into practice. This has a steadying and stabilising impact on the whole of society.

   Other valid answers will be accepted.

77 The family in the ummah

1. One mark will be awarded for each point identified up to a maximum of three marks. (3)
   - It is the duty of the ummah as Muslims to care for each other (1).
   - It shows unity between all Muslims (1).
   - It is a Muslim duty to provide guidance for the family in times of conflict (1).
   - Muslims believe that support from the ummah will lead to successful Muslim families who will, in turn, give stability to society (1).
   - It strengthens the ummah (1).

   Other valid answers will be accepted.

2. One mark will be awarded for providing each way and a second mark for development of the way up to a maximum of four marks. (4)
   - Muslims in the community can encourage families to worship together in their local mosque (1). This will unite them in a common shared goal of worshipping Allah (1).
   - The local community can provide parenting classes to support the family unit (1). These classes give parents guidance and support in how to raise their children (1).
   - The local community can provide counselling (1). This allows all members of the family unit to work together to resolve any issues (1).

   Other valid answers will be accepted.

78 Contraception

1. "Muslims should not use contraception." Be sure to make your points specific, and refer to teachings and views, as you are instructed. You can support your arguments with Qur'anic or other teachings. Make sure you give balanced views and then draw a conclusion – make sure you say why this is your conclusion. (12)

   Arguments for the statement:
   - Some Muslims believe that they should only use natural methods of contraception as promoted in some sources of authority in Islam. The use of artificial methods of contraception is not permitted.
   - Muslims believe that the purpose of sex is procreation – to have a family. Some Muslims believe that as permanent methods of contraception prevent this, they should not be used.
   - Many Muslims believe that having a family is a duty from Allah and so using contraception goes against this: 'when a husband and wife share intimacy it is rewarded, and a blessing from Allah.' (Hadith)

   Arguments against the statement:
   - Some Muslims believe that contraception can be used if there is a valid reason. This may include situations where the life of the mother could be at risk if she were to have a child; in this case, the use of contraception would be justified.
   - Some Muslims argue that using contraception in order to preserve current children would be a valid reason. If the wellbeing of the current family unit is protected through a couple using contraception, this would justify its use.
   - There are examples in Sahih al-Bukhari which teach that, in the time of Muhammad, natural forms of contraception were commonly used and so may be acceptable: 'we used to practise coitus interruptus during the lifetime of Allah's Apostle.'

   Other valid answers will be accepted.

79 Divorce

1. One mark will be awarded for providing each reason and a second mark for development of the reason up to a maximum of four marks. (4)
   - Muhammad taught that divorce should be a last resort (1). The couple are expected to try to reconcile before considering divorce (1).
   - Divorce is considered detestable by Allah (1). The Qur'an teaches that it is the most hated of all acts to Allah (1).
   - Marriage is intended to be for life (1). When a Muslim couple marry, they enter the union believing that it should last forever (1).

   Other valid answers will be accepted.

2. One mark will be awarded for providing each reason and a second mark for development of the reason up to a maximum of four marks. One further mark will be awarded for any relevant source of wisdom and authority. (5)
   - The Qur'an has strict guidelines on what should happen if a couple are considering divorce (1). Part of this process is the iddah, where there is a waiting period to see if a couple can reconcile (1): 'if they return (change their idea in this period), verily, Allah is Oft-Forgiving, Most Merciful.' (Surah 2:226) (1)

- Some Muslims are realistic and know that relationships can break down (1). As Muslims often have arranged marriages, there may be issues within a relationship that can lead to divorce (1): 'And if they decide upon divorce, then Allah is All-Hearer, All-Knower.' (Surah 2:227) (1)
- Shari'ah law teaches that divorce is allowed (1). Islam understands marriage to be a contract, so it can be ended (1): 'Then when they are about to fulfil their term appointed, either take them back in a good manner or part with them in a good manner.' (Surah 65:2)

Other valid answers will be accepted.

80 Men and women in the family

1. "Muslim men and women have equal roles in the family." Be sure to make your points specific, and refer to teachings and views, as you are instructed. You can support your arguments with Qur'anic or other teachings. Make sure you give balanced views and then draw a conclusion – make sure you say why this is your conclusion. (12)

   Arguments for the statement:
   - Muslims accept that men and woman have equal roles in the family, although these roles are different. Traditionally, men are seen as the providers and protectors, while women are the carers in the family and home.
   - Teachings from the Qur'an support the view of men and women having equality in the family: Surah 4 teaches that men and women were created 'from a single person' (Surah 4:1), which suggests equality, although this does not mean that they perform the exact same roles within the family unit.
   - Muhammad stood up for equality between men and women and his teaching supports the view of men and women having equal roles within the family. He taught that men and women were 'equal like the teeth of a comb' (Hadith), suggesting that although they perform different roles within the family, these roles complement each other.

   Arguments against the statement:
   - Some quotes in the Qur'an suggest there is inequality between men and women, supporting the view that women in the family must submit to their husbands: 'men are in charge of women' (Surah 4:34). This suggests that the roles of men and women are not equal and that men have power over women.
   - In the time of Muhammad, it is believed he witnessed many examples of inequality between men and women in the family. This may, for some Muslims, justify women not being seen or treated as equal within the family unit today.
   - In Islam, men and women are viewed by Muslims to be equal but not the same. Men are seen as the providers within the family unit, while women are regarded as the home-keepers and carers for children.

   Other valid answers will be accepted.

81 Gender prejudice and discrimination

1. One mark will be awarded for each point identified up to a maximum of three marks. (3)
   - Malala Yousafzai stood up against the Taliban to achieve equality in education (1).
   - Nadiya Hussain has raised awareness of the importance of gender equality (1).
   - Sisters in Islam challenge the mistreatment of women (1).
   - The Inclusive Mosque Initiative works for equality in prayer (1).
   - Many Muslims work to educate others about gender equality in Islam (1).

   Other valid answers will be accepted.

2. One mark will be awarded for providing each reason and a second mark for development of the reason up to a maximum of four marks. (4)
   - Islam teaches that men and women should be treated the same way (1). Muslims believe Allah created all humans to be equal (1).
   - Muslims believe that after death Allah will judge men and women in the same way (1). They believe that if a person – male or female – has acted as Allah wishes, they will be rewarded with entry to heaven (1).
   - Men and women have the same rights and responsibilities (1), for example men and women are both expected to get married (1).

   Other valid answers will be accepted.

UNIT 3: LIVING THE MUSLIM LIFE

82 The Ten Obligatory Acts of Shi'a Islam

1. One mark will be awarded for each point identified up to a maximum of three marks. (3)
   - One purpose of the Ten Obligatory Acts is to guide Shi'a Muslims in how they live their lives (1).
   - One purpose is to allow them to get closer to Allah (1).
   - One purpose is to help them reach paradise after death (1).
   - One purpose is to help them continually focus their actions on Allah (1).
   - One purpose is to unite all Shi'a Muslims in their shared beliefs (1).

   Other valid answers will be accepted.

2. One mark will be awarded for providing each way and a second mark for development of the way up to a maximum of four marks. (4)
   - Muslims must pray five times a day as one of the Ten Obligatory Acts (1). They believe that regular communication with Allah through daily worship fulfils the duty of Salah, which is one of the Ten Obligatory Acts (1).
   - Muslims try to resist temptations that may challenge them in their daily lives. (1) This could include not lying, swearing or harming others (1).
   - Muslims fast during the month of Ramadan (1). During this time, they do not eat or drink during daylight hours (1).

   Other valid answers will be accepted.

83 The Shahadah

1. One mark will be awarded for each point identified up to a maximum of three marks. (3)
   - The Shahadah contains the fundamental belief that there is one God (1).
   - The Shahadah contains the important belief that Muhammad is the prophet of Islam (1).
   - The Shahadah is accepted by all Muslims (1).
   - Muslims recite the Shahadah daily as a declaration of their faith (1).
   - Reciting the Shahadah is seen to demonstrate commitment to the religion of Islam (1).

   Other valid answers will be accepted.

2. One mark will be awarded for providing each way and a second mark for development of the way up to a maximum of four marks. (4)
   - The Shahadah is whispered into the ears of newborn babies (1). Muslims believe it is important that the first thing a baby hears is the idea of belief in one God, Allah (1).
   - Muslims believe it is important to say the Shahadah aloud in front of witnesses (1). This is done publicly so Muslims can show that they accept their religion, meaning they believe in Allah and Muhammad (1).
   - Muslims recite and hear the Shahadah daily (1). It is part of the adhan – the daily call to prayer (1).

   Other valid answers will be accepted.

84 Salah

1. "Salah is the most important of the Five Pillars for Muslims." Be sure to make your points specific, and refer to teachings and views, as you are instructed. You can support your arguments with Qur'anic or other teachings. Make sure you give balanced views and then draw a conclusion – make sure you say why this is your conclusion. In this question, 3 of

the marks awarded will be for your spelling, punctuation and grammar, and your use of specialist terminology. (15)

Arguments for the statement:
- Salah is compulsory prayer five times a day, which demonstrates regular communication with Allah. As it is one of the Five Pillars – which are duties – and it happens most frequently, some Muslims could consider it to be the most important of all the pillars.
- In performing Salah, all Muslims complete this pillar at the same time each day, facing the same way and performing the same actions, therefore uniting and strengthening the ummah. This might make it the most important pillar. Its importance is also shown through group communal prayer in the Jummah service, which takes place on a Friday in the mosque and which all Muslims strive to attend to show commitment to the ummah.
- Muhammad, as the prophet of Allah, established Salah and this shows its importance. The Qur'an states that Muhammad was the one who established prayer (Surah 29:45), demonstrating that he gave this special significance among the Five Pillars.

Arguments against the statement:
- Muslims might consider that no pillar is more important than any of the others. The basic beliefs and duties of Islam, collected together as the Five Pillars, are all equally important and Muslims believe all should be performed for Allah.
- Some Muslims may believe that Zakah and Sawm have more of a practical impact in the world and strengthen the ummah in a greater way than the other pillars. As Zakah and Sawm can involve helping others in the community through sharing money and food, they could be considered more important.
- Shahadah – the declaration of faith and the first Pillar of Islam – could be considered more important than prayer. Islam is understood by Muslims to mean 'submission to Allah', and as the Shahadah contains the belief that there is no God but Allah, it underpins all the other pillars and is regarded as most important for many Muslims.

Other valid answers will be accepted.

85 Sawm

1 One mark will be awarded for each point identified up to a maximum of three marks. (3)
- Muslims who are sick may be excused from fasting (1).
- Those who are elderly may be excused from fasting (1).
- Young children are excused from fasting (1).
- Pregnant women are excused from fasting (1).
- Those travelling on long journeys are excused from fasting (1).

Other valid answers will be accepted.

2 One mark will be awarded for providing each reason and a second mark for development of the reason up to a maximum of four marks. (4)
- Sawm is one of the Five Pillars and is therefore a duty (1). Fasting during Ramadan shows obedience to Allah (1).
- Performing Sawm shows self-discipline (1). Muslims must not eat during daylight hours, which shows that they are willing to suffer for Islam (1).
- Performing Sawm helps Muslims to remember the significance of the month of Ramadan in Islam (1). This was when the Qur'an was revealed to Muhammad from Allah (1).

Other valid answers will be accepted.

86 Zakah and khums

1 One mark will be awarded for each point identified up to a maximum of three marks. (3)
- Zakah is 2.5 per cent of a Muslim's annual wealth (1).
- Zakah is used to help the poor (1).
- Zakah is a duty in Islam (1).
- Zakah happens once a year (1).
- The act of giving Zakah is seen to strengthen and support the ummah (1).

Other valid answers will be accepted.

2 One mark will be awarded for providing each reason and a second mark for development of the reason up to a maximum of four marks. (4)
- Khums is important as it is used to directly support Muhammad's descendants and the leaders that Shi'a Muslims recognise as following him (1). The Qur'an details who should receive khums and how the money should be shared out (Surah 8) (1).
- Khums is important as it can be used to help those studying the religion of Islam (1). Khums is therefore used to benefit the whole religion of Islam, which in turn strengthens the ummah (1).
- Giving khums is important as Shi'a Muslims believe it is a duty (1). Shi'a Muslims recognise it as one of the Ten Obligatory Acts (1).

Other valid answers will be accepted.

87 Hajj

1 "The benefits of attending Hajj outweigh the challenges." Be sure to make your points specific, and refer to teachings and views, as you are instructed. You can support your arguments with Qur'anic or other teachings. Make sure you give balanced views and then draw a conclusion – make sure you say why this is your conclusion. In this question, 3 of the marks awarded will be for your spelling, punctuation and grammar, and your use of specialist terminology. (15)

Arguments for the statement:
- Hajj is one of the Five Pillars of Islam and is therefore a duty commanded by Allah, as seen in Surah 22. Muslims believe that by completing Hajj, they are demonstrating their commitment to Allah and to the religion of Islam.
- All Muslims are expected to try to complete Hajj once in their lifetime and it reinforces the view that all Muslims belong to the ummah. Completing Hajj reinforces ideas of equality with all Muslims wearing the same clothing and performing the same actions at the same time, so helping them to feel united and strengthening the ummah.
- Hajj is important for reminding Muslims of significant historical events in the religion of Islam detailed in the Qur'an (Surah 2). While completing this pillar, Muslims have the opportunity to focus on their religion, spending time in reflection and asking Allah for forgiveness, which is considered important if they are to achieve paradise after death.

Arguments against the statement:
- Muslims are expected to be physically fit and financially stable in order to complete Hajj and this can be a great challenge for some. Muslims may feel that they have failed Allah if they are not able to perform all Five Pillars, which are viewed as duties in the religion of Islam.
- One of the challenges of Hajj today is that it has become more popular, leading to over two million pilgrims attending every year. This can detract from the specialness of this event. Some Muslims may feel that there are too many people present to be able to have the personal experience of Allah they hope to achieve by completing this pillar.
- One of the greatest challenges of Hajj is that, recently, there have been many accidents in Makkah due to the large numbers of Muslims attending. The possibility of being killed may put off some Muslims who wish to complete all of the Five Pillars but feel Hajj is too dangerous.

Other valid answers will be accepted.

88 Jihad

1. One mark will be awarded for each point identified up to a maximum of three marks. (3)
   - Greater jihad is an inner struggle to be a better Muslim (1).
   - Greater jihad involves Muslims resisting temptation in their daily lives (1).
   - Muslims believe they can perform greater jihad by studying the Qur'an (1).
   - Muslims believe they can perform greater jihad by helping people in their local community (1).
   - Muslims believe they can perform greater jihad by attending the mosque regularly (1).
   Other valid answers will be accepted.

2. One mark will be awarded for providing each way and a second mark for development of the way up to a maximum of four marks. (4)
   - Jihad can be interpreted as greater jihad (1). This means that Muslims resist daily temptations in their lives (1).
   - One aspect of greater jihad can be understood as helping others (1). The ummah is seen as important in Islam in supporting Muslims all over the world (1).
   - Jihad can be understood as lesser jihad (1). This is understood as fighting in the name of Allah (1).
   Other valid answers will be accepted.

89 Celebrations and commemorations

1. "Celebrating festivals such as Id-ul Adha is vital in Islam." Be sure to make your points specific, and refer to teachings and views, as you are instructed. You can support your arguments with Qur'anic or other teachings. Make sure you give balanced views and then draw a conclusion – make sure you say why this is your conclusion. In this question, 3 of the marks awarded will be for your spelling, punctuation and grammar, and your use of specialist terminology. (15)
   Arguments for the statement:
   - Id-ul Adha is significant today as it is still celebrated by Muslims at the end of Hajj. Id-ul Adha is the Festival of Sacrifice, signifying the completion of the Fifth Pillar of Islam, and it is celebrated with a special service, cards and gifts.
   - Id-ul Adha continues to be significant today as it commemorates Ibrahim's willingness to sacrifice his son – a story from the Qur'an (Surah 37). This event shows how Ibrahim's faith was tested and Muslims believe they can learn from this and apply its meaning to their own lives.
   - Festivals such as Id-ul Adha help to strengthen the ummah by uniting all Muslims. A key element of the festival is sacrificing and sharing an animal with the poor.
   Arguments against the statement:
   - Some Muslims may believe that celebrating Id-ul Adha is outdated as it recalls events that happened a long time ago. They may argue that the focus should be on the development of Islam in the world today rather than remembering the history of the religion.
   - Some Muslims may recognise the celebration of Id-ul Adha as having some significance today, but also accept that other more practical celebrations in Islam can have a bigger impact in the world. Helping the poor – considered a duty – and giving money in Zakah, the Third Pillar of Islam, may have a bigger impact on uniting the ummah and caring for the poor than celebrating Id-ul Adha.
   - Some Muslims may view festivals such as Id-ul Adha as materialistic and not what the religion of Islam is about. They may feel that the central part of Islam is being close to Allah, which can be achieved in other ways, such as praying regularly or attending the mosque with other Muslims.
   Other valid answers will be accepted.

UNIT 4: MATTERS OF LIFE AND DEATH

90 Origins of the universe

1. One mark will be awarded for each point identified up to a maximum of three marks. (3)
   - Everything was created by Allah (1).
   - Balance was created in the universe (1).
   - Creation took periods of time (1).
   - Creation was planned by Allah (1).
   - Humans were created by Allah (1).
   Other valid answers will be accepted.

2. One mark will be awarded for providing each response and a second mark for development of the response up to a maximum of four marks. (4)
   - Some Muslims believe that science and Islam together explain how the universe was created (1). The 'Big Bang' explains how Allah created the universe (1).
   - Some Muslims do not see any conflict between Islam and scientific explanations (1). They believe that scientific explanations help them to understand Allah's creation (1).
   - Some Muslims view science and Islam as in conflict (1). The 'Big Bang' conflicts with the idea of Allah creating the universe (1).
   Other valid answers will be accepted.

91 Sanctity of life

1. One mark will be awarded for each point identified up to a maximum of three marks. (3)
   - All life was created by Allah (1).
   - Life should be respected (1).
   - All humans have equal worth (1).
   - Only Allah can take life away (1).
   - Life is sacred (1).
   Other valid answers will be accepted.

2. One mark will be awarded for providing each reason and a second mark for development of the reason up to a maximum of four marks. (4)
   - Muslims believe human life is holy because it was created by Allah (1). They believe it should be respected as it was made to be sacred (1).
   - Humans were given responsibilities directly from Allah, showing they are different from all other creations (1). Humans were made to be khalifahs or stewards for Allah (1).
   - Muslims believe human life is holy as the Qur'an contains teachings suggesting that the taking of life is wrong (1): 'whoever kills a soul … it is as if he had slain mankind entirely.' (Surah 5:32) (1)
   Other valid answers will be accepted.

92 The origins of human life

1. "It is possible to accept both evolution and Islamic ideas about the origin of human life." Be sure to make your points specific, and refer to teachings and views, as you are instructed. You can support your arguments with Qur'anic or other teachings. Make sure you give balanced views and then draw a conclusion – make sure you say why this is your conclusion. (12)
   Arguments for the statement:
   - Some Muslims argue that evolution was part of Allah's plan for creating humans and so bring Islamic ideas and science together. They believe that evolution explains how Allah created humans so that the strongest characteristics survived.
   - Many Muslims believe that science has more evidence and is more believable than earlier arguments about the origins of humans. They believe that although sources of authority such as the Qur'an are not wrong, they do need to adapt beliefs to the changing scientific world.
   - Many Muslims believe it is possible for science to offer a fuller explanation alongside Islam of how humans were

created by Allah. The two are not in conflict as science is able to develop Islamic beliefs about this topic and allows Muslims to understand better how human life was created.
Arguments against the statement:
- Qur'anic explanations of Allah's 'creation of man from clay' (Surah 32:7) appear to be in direct conflict with the theory of evolution, leaving no common ground between the two standpoints.
- Some Muslims believe that there are too many differences between science and Islam and therefore reject all ideas that appear to conflict with traditional Islamic beliefs. Muslims want to believe that Allah planned and designed humans to be special, not that humans developed by adapting to their environments as the theory of evolution claims.
- The Qur'an reinforces the view that Allah is the sole creator and designer of human life and that he did this without help, which contradicts scientific explanations. The Qur'an claims that Allah 'made from water every living thing.' (Surah 21:30)

Other valid answers will be accepted.

93 Muslim attitudes to abortion

1   One mark will be awarded for providing each reason and a second mark for development of the reason up to a maximum of four marks. (4)
    - Some Muslims do not accept abortion as they believe in the sanctity of life (1). Life is regarded as sacred because it was created by Allah (1).
    - Some Muslims do not accept abortion as they believe it is against the Qur'an's teaching: 'And kill not your children for fear of poverty' (Surah 17:31) (1). Muslims believe only Allah can give and take life (1).
    - Some Muslims believe abortion is wrong because Allah gives each person a soul (1): 'the soul is breathed into his body.' (Sahih al-Bukhari 55:549) (1)

    Other valid answers will be accepted.

2   One mark will be awarded for providing each reason and a second mark for development of the reason up to a maximum of four marks. (4)
    - Some Muslims would respond by arguing that abortion is not acceptable due to the sanctity of life (1). Muslims believe life is sacred as it was created by Allah (1).
    - Some Muslims would respond by arguing that abortion is always wrong because the Qur'an teaches 'And kill not your children for fear of poverty' (Surah 17:31) (1). Muslims believe only Allah can give and take life (1).
    - Some Muslims may respond by arguing that there are some circumstances when abortion would be permitted if it protected the sanctity of the life of the mother (1), for example if the mother had been raped or if her health were put at risk (1).

    Other valid answers will be accepted.

94 Death and the afterlife (1)

1   One mark will be awarded for providing each reason and a second mark for development of the reason up to a maximum of four marks. (4)
    - The Qur'an contains many teachings stating that there is an afterlife (1). Surah 28 talks of the idea of resurrection (Surah 28:61) (1).
    - Muslims are taught that one of the characteristics of Allah is that he will judge them after death (1). Surah 39 says 'And to every soul will be paid in full (the fruit) of its Deeds.' (Surah 39:70) (1)
    - Muslims believe that having a reward or punishment in the afterlife seems fair and just (1). Islam teaches of the existence of paradise where the good will be rewarded and hell where people will be punished (1).

    Other valid answers will be accepted.

2   One mark will be awarded for providing each teaching and a second mark for development of the teaching up to a maximum of four marks. One further mark will be awarded for any relevant source of wisdom and authority. (5)
    - The Qur'an talks of a 'Day of Resurrection' (Surah 28:61) (1). Islam teaches that on the Day of Resurrection Allah will judge humans on the way they have behaved during their lives on Earth (1): 'And to every soul will be paid in full (the fruit) of its Deeds.' (Surah 39:70) (1)
    - There are many verses in the Qur'an which refer to Allah as a judge (1). Muslims believe Allah will decide whether a person deserves to be rewarded or punished in the afterlife (1): 'those who have believed … shall be made happy … and those who have rejected Faith … shall be brought forth to Punishment.' (Surah 30:15–16) (1)
    - Muslims believe there is evidence in the Qur'an for a place of paradise for good people and a place of punishment for bad people (1): 'the Fire, which is prepared for the disbelievers.' (Surah 3:131) (1)

    Other valid answers will be accepted.

95 Death and the afterlife (2)

1   "Everyone should believe in life after death." Be sure to make your points specific, and refer to teachings and views, as you are instructed. You can support your arguments with Qur'anic or other teachings. Make sure you give balanced views and then draw a conclusion – make sure you say why this is your conclusion. (12)

    Arguments for the statement:
    - A belief in life after death is important as it helps Muslims to understand how they should live their lives. Accepting the idea of reward or punishment after death means that they must know how Allah wants them to live in order to be rewarded in paradise (al-Jannah).
    - There are many Muslim teachings on beliefs about life after death in sources of authority such as the Qur'an. Surah 28 talks of a 'Day of Resurrection' (Surah 28:61) when Allah will judge humans on the way they have behaved during their lives on Earth.
    - Muslims believe that after death Allah will judge them on the Day of Judgement. This is important as belief in akhirah gives their lives meaning and purpose, and will impact on their behaviour and the way they treat others.

    Arguments against the statement:
    - Many non-religious people do not accept life after death as there is no proof. They think that belief in an afterlife gives a false sense of hope and there is no scientific evidence that it exists as no one has ever returned to prove it.
    - Humanists believe there is no life after death: when a person dies their body just decays. They believe that life after death is impossible.
    - Non-religious people claim that some people have been tricked into believing in an afterlife. They think that the promise of an afterlife was used in the past to control people's behaviour through the fear of punishment, but today reason tells us there is no afterlife.

    Other valid answers will be accepted.

96 Euthanasia

1   One mark will be awarded for each point identified up to a maximum of three marks. (3)
    - Allah created life and only he can take it away, which makes euthanasia wrong (1).
    - The Qur'an teaches the sanctity of life as it is Allah's creation (1).
    - The Qur'an teaches that only Allah can decide how long a person's life will be (1).
    - Euthanasia is seen as suicide, which is not accepted in Islam (1).
    - Suffering is regarded as an accepted test of faith in Islam (1).

    Other valid answers will be accepted.

2   One mark will be awarded for providing each reason and a second mark for development of the reason up to a maximum of four marks. One further mark will be awarded for any relevant source of wisdom and authority. (5)

- Muslims do not accept euthanasia because they believe in the sanctity of life (1). The Qur'an teaches 'And do not kill yourselves (or one another)' (Surah 4:29) (1). This shows that life is special and sacred as it was created by Allah and, therefore, should not be ended by humans (1).
- Muslims believe euthanasia is wrong as all life is created by Allah (1). Muslims believe only Allah can decide when life begins and ends (1): 'Indeed we belong to Allah, and indeed to Him we will return.' (Surah 2:156) (1)
- Muslims do not accept euthanasia as the Qur'an teaches that it is seen as suicide (1). Islam teaches that ending your own life is against Allah (1): 'And no person can ever die except by Allah's Leave and at an appointed term.' (Surah 3:145) (1)
- Muslims believe euthanasia is wrong as Islam teaches that suffering has a purpose (1). Muslims believe that suffering may be a test of faith from Allah (1): 'Do the people think that they will be left to say, "We believe" and they will not be tried?' (Surah 29:2) (1)

Other valid answers will be accepted.

97 Issues in the natural world

1 "Muslims should protect animals." Be sure to make your points specific, and refer to teachings and views, as you are instructed. You can support your arguments with Qur'anic or other teachings. Make sure you give balanced views and then draw a conclusion – make sure you say why this is your conclusion. (12)

Arguments for the statement:
- Muslims may agree that animals should be protected as they believe the world is a gift Allah created for humans and should be respected. The Qur'an teaches: 'It is Allah who made for you the grazing animals upon which you ride, and some of them you eat' (Surah 40:79). This shows that although people can use animals and enjoy them, they are still Allah's creation.
- Muslims believe that they should protect animals because after death Allah will judge them on the way they have lived their lives. This includes the way they treated animals, so they should not mistreat or abuse them.
- Although Muslims believe the world was created by Allah, including the provision of animals as a gift to humanity, they also believe they were given the responsibility of being stewards (khalifahs). This means they believe that they should look after Allah's creation, including animals, and not exploit or abuse them.

Arguments against the statement:
- Many Muslims view humans as the ultimate part of Allah's creation. According to the sanctity of life argument, they were made to be special and different from animals, meaning that animals can be used by humans as they wish.
- Muslims may believe that Allah created animals for humans and therefore they do not need the protection of humans. Many Muslims are not vegetarian and eat meat, believing this is acceptable to Allah.
- Some Muslims may believe that as humans are superior to animals, animals can be used in experimentation if it will protect human life. Allah is believed to have given humans souls, making them sacred, whereas animals are not.

Other valid answers will be accepted.

UNIT 5: CRIME AND PUNISHMENT

98 Justice

1 "Justice is important for the victims of crime." Be sure to make your points specific, and refer to teachings and views, as you are instructed. You can support your arguments with Qur'anic or other teachings. Make sure you give balanced views and then draw a conclusion – make sure you say why this is your conclusion. (12)

Arguments for the statement:
- Islam teaches that justice is important for the victim. This is a key idea promoted in the Qur'an, which teaches Muslims to 'be persistently standing firm in justice' (Surah 4:135). This shows the importance of standing up for justice, including for that of the victim.
- Muslims believe that Islam is a religion based on justice because Allah himself is just. The Five Pillars teach Muslims to behave in a just way towards others. Providing justice for victims is in line with this idea and puts Muslim teachings into action.
- Muslims believe that after death they will be judged by Allah on the way they have lived their lives. Making sure that victims of crime receive justice is important in ensuring that everyone will be judged fairly on their actions after death.

Arguments against the statement:
- Some Muslims may believe that justice has a purpose wider than simply benefiting the victims of crime. Society in general, criminals and others who are possibly considering committing the same crime need to see that justice is being done and that there are consequences of crimes. This will help to maintain control in society.
- Many Muslims refer to Shari'ah law as their code of conduct when considering matters of justice. They would argue that following this law will provide justice for both the victim and also the offender – giving the criminal the opportunity to change and reform their behaviour.
- Muslims believe that equality is important and upholding justice can help to achieve this ideal. Although accepted for different reasons, in matters of crime all of those involved (victim, victim's family, offender and society) should be treated fairly and equally.

Other valid answers will be accepted.

99 Crime

1 One mark will be awarded for each point identified up to a maximum of three marks. (3)
- Islam teaches that crime is a distraction from Allah (1).
- Islam teaches that Allah knows all crimes committed (1).
- The Qur'an teaches that Allah orders justice (1).
- Islam teaches that criminals deserve to be treated fairly (1).
- Islam teaches that Muslims have a duty to help those who have committed crimes (1).

Other valid answers will be accepted.

2 One mark will be awarded for providing each way and a second mark for development of the way up to a maximum of four marks. (4)
- Organisations such as the Muslim Chaplains' Association work directly with prisoners (1). They support offenders after they are released and encourage them not to return to a life of crime (1).
- Organisations such as Mosaic operate a young offenders' programme (1). They educate young people about alternatives to a life of crime (1).
- Volunteers from the organisation Mosaic go into prisons to support young prisoners and to act as role models (1). They help them as they complete their prison sentences and look to rejoin society (1).

Other valid answers will be accepted.

100 Good, evil and suffering

1 One mark will be awarded for each point identified up to a maximum of three marks. (3)
- Islam teaches that Allah will reward Muslims who have followed his teachings in the afterlife (1).
- Muslims believe completing the Five Pillars of Islam will help them to achieve a reward in the afterlife (1).
- Islam teaches that helping others will help Muslims gain a reward in the afterlife (1).
- Islam teaches that the reward after death for good actions will be paradise for eternity (1).
- Islam teaches Muslims that Allah watches them and knows when they perform good actions (1).

Other valid answers will be accepted.

2. One mark will be awarded for providing each reason and a second mark for development of the reason up to a maximum of four marks. (4)
   - Muslims believe that suffering has a purpose from Allah (1). It is part of his plan and therefore should not be questioned (1).
   - Muslims believe that suffering may be a test of faith (1). It is a test of their commitment to Allah and the religion of Islam in the face of evil in the world (1).
   - Islam teaches that suffering is a reminder of Muslims' daily struggle to overcome temptation and evil (1). Muslims believe that suffering is sometimes the result of human actions when they do wrong (1).
   Other valid answers will be accepted.

101 Punishment

1. One mark will be awarded for providing each reason and a second mark for development of the reason up to a maximum of four marks. One further mark will be awarded for any relevant source of wisdom and authority. (5)
   - Muslims believe that justice in the form of fair punishment is important when crimes have been committed (1). The Qur'an promotes the idea of justice through the concept of reward and punishment after death (1): 'But whoever transgresses after that will have a painful punishment.' (Surah 2:178) (1)
   - Muslims also believe that the ummah requires stability in society, which can be achieved through just punishment when a crime has been committed (1). Both the Qur'an and Shari'ah law teach that Muslims should stand up for justice and fairness (1): 'O you who have believed, be persistently standing firm in justice, witnesses for Allah.' (Surah 4:135) (1)
   - Just punishment gives offenders the opportunity to understand why their behaviour was wrong and to mend their ways (1). Allah is forgiving (1): 'Allah is Ever All-Knowing, All-Wise. He will admit to His Mercy whom He will.' (Surah 76:30–31)
   Other valid answers will be accepted.

102 Aims of punishment

1. One mark will be awarded for each point identified up to a maximum of three marks. (3)
   - There are specific instructions in the Qur'an for particular crimes (1).
   - Punishment should be appropriate for the crime committed (1).
   - Punishment should bring justice (1).
   - Punishment should provide the chance to reform (1).
   - Punishment should deter others from committing the same crime (1).
   Other valid answers will be accepted.

2. One mark will be awarded for providing each reason and a second mark for development of the reason up to a maximum of four marks. (4)
   - Muslims believe the Qur'an teaches that Allah is merciful and offenders should be given the opportunity to understand the difference between right and wrong (1). This will also help to provide stability to the ummah and to reinforce some of the other aims of punishment, such as protecting society (1).
   - Muslims believe that forgiveness is important and that it gives criminals the chance to change their behaviour (1). Allah is believed to be just and forgiving, and Muslims believe that they should also develop these characteristics (1).
   - Muslims believe that Allah will judge people after death on their actions, so giving offenders the chance to change their behaviour will allow them to become better Muslims (1). Helping and forgiving others also helps Muslims to achieve their goal of attaining al-Jannah (1).
   Other valid answers will be accepted.

103 Forgiveness

1. "Criminals should always be forgiven." Be sure to make your points specific, and refer to teachings and views, as you are instructed. You can support your arguments with Qur'anic or other teachings. Make sure you give balanced views and then draw a conclusion – make sure you say why this is your conclusion. (12)
   Arguments for the statement:
   - The Qur'an teaches that Allah is merciful and forgiving, and Muslims believe that they should try to develop these characteristics in their own lives. Muslims should try to 'pardon and overlook, and forgive ...' (Surah 64:14).
   - Islam is considered by Muslims to be a religion of peace and they believe they should work together to create a peaceful world. Putting this into practice means forgiving people when they do things that are wrong, and accepting that they are sorry in order to make peace with them.
   - Muslims believe that after death they will be judged by Allah on the way they lived their lives. This includes showing forgiveness towards others and being sorry for wrongdoing in order to achieve a reward in al-Jannah with Allah.
   Arguments against the statement:
   - There may be some crimes it would be difficult to forgive. For example, if a member of a person's family was killed it might be difficult to forgive the offender, so some Muslims may feel that not all crimes can be forgiven.
   - Fair justice is an important idea promoted in the Qur'an: 'be persistently standing firm in justice, witnesses for Allah' (Surah 4:135). However, in some cases of justice it may be hard to show forgiveness, especially where an offender may not be sorry for the crime they have committed.
   - Some Muslims believe that Allah will judge them after death and that it is his place alone to be just and to forgive, especially in circumstances where violent crimes have been committed. They may believe that the law should punish criminals but that forgiveness should not necessarily be a part of this.
   Other valid answers will be accepted.

104 Treatment of criminals

1. One mark will be awarded for each point identified up to a maximum of three marks. (3)
   - Muslims believe criminals should be treated with justice (1).
   - Muslims believe criminals should be treated humanely (1).
   - Muslims believe criminals should be treated with respect (1).
   - Muslims believe criminals should have basic human rights (1).
   - Muslims believe criminals should not be tortured (1).
   Other valid answers will be accepted.

2. One mark will be awarded for providing each reason and a second mark for development of the reason up to a maximum of four marks. (4)
   - Muslims believe that all life – including that of prisoners – is sacred as it was created by Allah (1). The Qur'an teaches that all human life should be valued and respected, so prisoners should also have a right to life and recognition of their basic human rights (1).
   - Muslims believe that because Allah is just, they should also act justly towards prisoners (1). The Qur'an teaches 'be persistently standing firm in justice' (Surah 4:135), so it is fair for prisoners to have basic human rights, e.g. food and water (1).
   - Muslims believe that Allah will judge them after death on how they have behaved in life (1). Ensuring fair treatment of prisoners and recognising their basic human rights will help Muslims to achieve a reward in paradise (1).
   Other valid answers will be accepted.

105 The death penalty

1. "Everyone should support the use of the death penalty." Be sure to make your points specific, and refer to teachings and

views, as you are instructed. You can support your arguments with Qur'anic or other teachings. Make sure you give balanced views and then draw a conclusion – make sure you say why this is your conclusion. (12)

Arguments for the statement:
- There are teachings in Islam which suggest that the death penalty can be used for the crime of murder and for those who refuse to do their Islamic duty: 'in one of the three cases: the married adulterer, a life for life, and the deserter of his Din (Islam), abandoning the community … [the death penalty is permissible].' (Sahih Muslim Hadith 16:4152)
- Some Muslims may point to the teachings of Muhammad which suggest that he agreed with the use of the death penalty, therefore making it acceptable for some crimes. For example, Hadith 682 talks of Muhammad ordering the death of a woman adulteress.
- Shari'ah law is used by Muslims to apply Islamic teachings and to decide punishments for crimes. It agrees with the teachings in the Qur'an, supporting the view that the death penalty can be used for some serious crimes.

Arguments against the statement:
- Many Muslims believe that although the Qur'an justifies the use of the death penalty for some crimes, it is not the only possible punishment. They may suggest that, in today's society, other punishments may be more appropriate for crimes, allowing criminals to reform and be forgiven.
- Muslims believe in the sanctity of life, which states that human life is special and sacred as it was created by Allah and given a soul: 'Then the soul is breathed into his body' (Sahih al-Bukhari 55:549). It is therefore wrong to take life, and so many Muslims would not support the use of the death penalty.
- Non-religious people such as Humanists would not support the use of the death penalty, believing that it is possible for errors to occur and that some innocent people could be put to death.

Other valid answers will be accepted.

UNIT 6: PEACE AND CONFLICT

106 Peace

1 One mark will be awarded for each point identified up to a maximum of three marks. (3)
- 'Islam' comes from the word 'salaam', often understood to mean 'peace' (1).
- Muslims greet each other with messages of peace (1).
- Muslims promote peace through standing up for justice (1).
- All Muslims are part of the ummah, which promotes equality and peace (1).
- The Qur'an talks of Muslims using 'words of peace' (Surah 25:63) (1).

Other valid answers will be accepted.

2 One mark will be awarded for providing each reason and a second mark for development of the reason up to a maximum of four marks. (4)
- The Qur'an teaches that Muslims should use 'words of peace' (Surah 25:63) (1). This shows that peace is important even when facing hatred or criticism from others (1).
- All Muslims are part of the ummah, which unites them in peace (1). Islam teaches Muslims that they have a duty from Allah to support and care for each other in peace (1).
- Muslims are taught to achieve justice in the world peacefully (1). Justice is a key idea taught in the Qur'an, with Muslims encouraged to remain 'standing firm in justice, witnesses for Allah.' (Surah 4:135) (1)

Other valid answers will be accepted.

107 Peacemaking

1 One mark will be awarded for providing each way and a second mark for development of the way up to a maximum of four marks. (4)

- The Muslim Peace Fellowship promotes ideas of peace in the world through education (1). It holds conferences and talks to demonstrate unity and peace between different religions (1).
- The Muslim Peace Fellowship reaches out to people of all faiths to work to reduce injustice in the world so that people can live in peace (1). It raises awareness of the situation of refugees and provides practical help to make society fairer and more peaceful (1).
- Islamic Relief provides emergency relief and aid in war-torn countries so peace can be restored (1). It provides medical care, food and water to relieve suffering and works to achieve peace between different groups (1).

Other valid answers will be accepted.

2 One mark will be awarded for providing each reason and a second mark for development of the reason up to a maximum of four marks. (4)
- Surah 41 talks of the importance of forgiveness and reconciliation in bringing peace to the world (Surah 41:34) (1). The Qur'an teaches that Allah created a world with the intention of people living together in peace (1).
- Islam teaches that Muslims have a duty to care for each other and to bring peace to the world (1). All Muslims are part of the ummah and are expected to look after and to support each other in peace (1).
- Many key teachings, beliefs and ideas in Islam are related to people living in peace with each other (1). The Five Pillars includes the concept of giving money in Zakah to help the poor and to create a fairer and more peaceful society (1).

Other valid answers will be accepted.

108 Conflict

1 One mark will be awarded for each point identified up to a maximum of three marks. (3)
- Muslims work to bring peace to groups in conflict (1).
- Muslims educate others to respect the equality of all as part of the ummah (1).
- Muslims work towards reconciliation through forgiveness (1).
- Some Muslims may fight as a last resort to restore peace (1).
- Some Muslims may fight to defend their religion (1).

Other valid answers will be accepted.

2 One mark will be awarded for providing each teaching and a second mark for development of the teaching up to a maximum of four marks. One further mark will be awarded for any relevant source of wisdom and authority. (5)
- The Qur'an teaches that it may be justified under certain conditions to fight in order to bring about the goal of peace, which is important to Muslims (1). Muslims recognise that fighting should be a last resort but that it can bring peace (1): 'And what is [the matter] with you that you fight not in the cause of Allah and [for] the oppressed among men, women, and children …' (Surah 4:75) (1).
- Islam teaches that any fighting that does happen should be fair and just (1). Muslims believe that Allah is just and that this should be applied to all situations, even war (1): 'Fight in the way of Allah those who fight you but do not transgress. Indeed, Allah does not like transgressors.' (Surah 2:190) (1)
- Islam teaches the importance of peace and forgiveness when faced with conflict (1). Muslims believe they should work to find peaceful solutions and to forgive others rather than fight (1): 'And the servants of the Most Merciful are those who walk upon the earth easily, and when the ignorant address them [harshly], they say [words of] peace.' (Surah 25:63) (1)

Other valid answers will be accepted.

109 Pacifism

1 "Muslims should all be pacifists." Be sure to make your points specific, and refer to teachings and views, as you are instructed. You can support your arguments with Qur'anic or other teachings. Make sure you give balanced views and then draw a conclusion – make sure you say why this is your conclusion. (12)

Arguments for the statement:
- Some Muslims may agree with this statement, believing that Islam is a religion of peace and that putting this into practice in the world can best be done through being pacifist. There are many teachings on peace in the Qur'an, showing that violence is not the answer.
- Some Muslims believe that they should be pacifists and work to achieve justice in the world because the Qur'an teaches that Allah created a world where people should live in peace together. This can only be achieved through peaceful means such as pacifism.
- The Qur'an stresses the importance of reconciliation and of working together to achieve unity – Surah 41 talks of justice, forgiveness and reconciliation helping to bring about peace. The ummah also demonstrates this as Muslims believe they have a duty to care and support all Muslims in the world and to work together for peace.

Arguments against the statement:
- Some Muslims may disagree with this statement as Islam is not traditionally associated with pacifism. Muhammad was forced to flee Makkah and there is evidence that he was forced to use violence, thus going against ideas of pacifism.
- Islam teaches in the Qur'an that sometimes violence is necessary in order to achieve peace, thus going against ideas of pacifism: 'Fight in the way of Allah those who fight you' (Surah 2:190). This recognises that there are cases where violence is sometimes justified in order to bring about peace.
- Warfare has been a part of Islam since the time of Muhammad, which goes against the principles of pacifism. Muhammad fought in the Battle of Badr and, more recently, the concept of lesser jihad has been used to justify the use of violence in defence of Islam.

Other valid answers will be accepted.

110 The Just War theory

1. One mark will be awarded for each point identified up to a maximum of three marks. (3)
   - War should not target innocents (1).
   - War should always be a last resort (1).
   - War should only be fought when agreed by the whole community (1).
   - War should not be fought to win land or power (1).
   - War should always be an act of defence (1).

   Other valid answers will be accepted.

2. One mark will be awarded for providing each way and a second mark for development of the way up to a maximum of four marks. (4)
   - Some Muslims may recognise that war is sometimes necessary (1). They believe that the Just War theory considers war to be a last resort and supports the idea of protecting innocent life (1).
   - Shi'a Muslims recognise lesser jihad (Just War) as one of the Ten Obligatory Acts (1). They believe the conditions of Just War theory ensure that war is fought for the right reasons and in the right way (1).
   - Sunni Muslims do not place great emphasis on Just War theory (1). They may believe that reconciliation and forgiveness are at the heart of Islam and therefore believe that no war is justified (1).

   Other valid answers will be accepted.

111 Holy war

1. One mark will be awarded for each point identified up to a maximum of three marks. (3)
   - The Qur'an suggests that violence can be used if necessary (1).
   - The Qur'an teaches the importance of peace and not war (Surah 8) (1).
   - The Qur'an teaches that forgiveness should be shown if the opposition repents (Surah 9) (1).
   - Holy war is justifiable in order to defend Islam (Surah 4) (1).
   - The Qur'an suggests that Muslims should not attack others without good cause (Surah 2) (1).

   Other valid answers will be accepted.

2. One mark will be awarded for providing each reason and a second mark for development of the reason up to a maximum of four marks. (4)
   - The Qur'an teaches that violence can be used when it is considered necessary (Surah 9) (1). One of the conditions of holy war is that it be fought for the defence of Islam (1).
   - One condition of holy war is to protect human life, which the Qur'an teaches is special (1). Muslims believe that human life is sacred as it was created by Allah (1).
   - Holy war is accepted by Muslims if it is fought fairly and with justice (1). Muslims believe that Allah is just and fair, and the Qur'an encourages Muslims to act justly towards others, even in war (Surah 2) (1).

   Other valid answers will be accepted.

112 Weapons of mass destruction

1. "Weapons of mass destruction should never be used." Be sure to make your points specific, and refer to teachings and views, as you are instructed. You can support your arguments with Qur'anic or other teachings. Make sure you give balanced views and then draw a conclusion – make sure you say why this is your conclusion. (12)

   Arguments for the statement:
   - Muslims believe that although the Qur'an doesn't say anything directly about the use of weapons of mass destruction (WMD), its teachings can be interpreted to show that they are wrong. The Qur'an suggests that if any person is killed, it would be like the killing of all mankind, showing that taking the life of others using WMD is wrong: 'whoever kills a soul … it is as if he had slain mankind entirely.' (Surah 5:32)
   - Muslims support the sanctity of life theory, which is the idea that life is special and sacred as it is created by Allah. WMD threaten human life, causing the deaths of innocents, and their use therefore cannot be justified as it goes against this teaching.
   - WMD cannot be justified due to the destruction they cause to the environment, which Muslims accept is the creation of Allah. The Qur'an teaches that Allah's creation should be respected and that humans are given the responsibility of being khalifahs, with a duty to care for the world. This would involve not supporting the use of WMD.

   Arguments against the statement:
   - Some people may support the use of WMD, using the ethical theory of utilitarianism as their justification. This ethical theory works on the principle of 'the greatest happiness for the greatest number' and the use of WMD could be justified if they are used as a deterrent to prevent war.
   - Some people may support the use of WMD to bring about a quicker end to conflict. With traditional forms of warfare, each side could be evenly balanced in terms of conflict but with WMD one side might have an advantage and therefore a sustained and lengthy conflict could be prevented.
   - Some people may support the use of WMD to minimise casualties on the side of those who use them. WMD give great power and advantage to the side that has them; they cause far more destruction and death than traditional methods of warfare.

   Other valid answers will be accepted.

113 Issues surrounding conflict

1. One mark will be awarded for each point identified up to a maximum of three marks. (3)
   - The Muslim Council of Britain runs education programmes. (1).
   - Muslims can be involved in interfaith groups that work together to end conflict (1).
   - Muslims can be involved in peaceful rallies to protest against conflict (1).

- Muslims can be part of organisations such as Mosaic, which works to reduce conflict (1).
- Muslims can take part in charity work to help those suffering as a result of conflict (1).

Other valid answers will be accepted.

2 One mark will be awarded for providing each way and a second mark for development of the way up to a maximum of four marks. (4)
- Some Muslims may be involved in charity work to help those suffering as a result of conflict (1). They could be part of an organisation such as Islamic Relief, which works to bring aid to people in places of conflict (1).
- Some Muslims may speak out against those who commit atrocities in the world (1), for example the Muslim Council of Britain has spoken out after Islamic extremist attacks (1).
- Some Muslims may work to educate people about the peaceful messages Islam promotes (1). They could become involved in an interfaith group that helps to find common ground between religions and works to bring an end to conflict (1).

Other valid answers will be accepted.

UNIT 7: PHILOSOPHY OF RELIGION

114 Revelation

1 One mark will be awarded for each point identified up to a maximum of three marks. (3)
- Allah chooses to reveal himself directly through the Qur'an (1).
- Muslims believe that they can understand what Allah is like through the Qur'an (1).
- Muslims believe the Qur'an is proof of Allah's existence (1).
- Muslims believe the Qur'an reveals how Allah wants them to live their lives (1).
- Muslims believe the Qur'an reveals Allah is omnipotent (1).

Other valid answers will be accepted.

2 One mark will be awarded for each point identified up to a maximum of three marks. (3)
- The Qur'an shows that Allah is omnipotent (1).
- The Qur'an shows that Allah is omniscient (1).
- The Qur'an shows that Allah is benevolent (1).
- The Qur'an shows that Allah is transcendent (1).
- The Qur'an shows that Allah is immanent (1).

Other valid answers will be accepted.

115 Visions

1 One mark will be awarded for providing each reason and a second mark for development of the reason up to a maximum of four marks. (4)
- Visions show Muslims that Allah is all-powerful and are proof that he exists (1). For example, Allah spoke to Musa in a vision in order to communicate with humanity (1).
- Muslims believe that Allah's nature is revealed in visions such as the one Mary received (1). The Qur'anic account reveals that Allah is merciful and chose Mary to be the mother of Isa (Surah 19:16–20) (1).
- Many Muslims believe that Allah is transcendent and cannot therefore be seen directly, so visions help to connect him to humanity (1). This can be seen in the example of Moses (Surah 7) (1).

Other valid answers will be accepted.

2 One mark will be awarded for providing each reason and a second mark for development of the reason up to a maximum of four marks. (4)
- Some Muslims prefer to look to other sources of revelation that they feel offer stronger proof of Allah's existence (1). The Qur'an is a direct source of revelation from Allah and tells Muslims about the nature of Allah, as well as being proof of his existence (1).
- Some Muslims believe that having faith in Allah means having trust without proof (1). Shi'a Muslims hold this point of view (1).
- Some Muslims believe that Allah is transcendent and too great to be fully understood through visions (1). For example, in the Qur'an the vision experienced by Musa was not a direct vision of Allah (1).

Other valid answers will be accepted.

116 Miracles

1 "Miracles are evidence of Allah's existence." Be sure to make your points specific, and refer to teachings and views, as you are instructed. You can support your arguments with Qur'anic or other teachings. Make sure you give balanced views and then draw a conclusion – make sure you say why this is your conclusion. (12)

Arguments for the statement:
- The Qur'an is a source of authority for Muslims because it is given to them by Allah; including miracles in the Qur'an gives them significance. Examples of miracles such as Nuh and the flood help to strengthen the argument that Allah exists.
- Muslims believe that miracles demonstrate the nature of Allah and, in turn, prove that he exists. Miracles demonstrate Allah's power over and love for the world. They allow him to connect with humanity in order to reveal what he is like and to confirm his existence.
- Many Muslims believe that miracles allow them to understand Allah better and to become closer to him. Miracles are evidence of Allah working within the world and examples such as Al-Mi'raj – where Muhammad was taken to meet Allah – reinforce the fact that he exists.

Arguments against the statement:
- Some Muslims do not place great emphasis on miracles as proof of the existence of Allah. Instead, they may see the example of Muhammad as a prophet or the Qur'an itself as more significant sources of authority in strengthening their view that Allah exists.
- Non-religious people might offer alternative explanations for miracles, thereby challenging whether they prove the existence of Allah. They might use science to show that miracles do not happen, and that events considered to be miraculous may have reasonable explanations that need no reference to Allah.
- Some Muslims may accept that miracles happen, but believe they are not necessary in order to have faith and belief in Allah. They may believe that having faith in Allah means trusting that he exists without needing further proof of this.

Other valid answers will be accepted.

117 Religious experiences

1 One mark will be awarded for each point identified up to a maximum of three marks. (3)
- Muslims believe that religious experiences reveal the nature of Allah (1).
- Muslims believe that religious experiences can take the form of visions (1).
- Muslims believe that religious experiences can take the form of miracles (1).
- Muslims believe that the Qur'an was revealed to Muhammad through a religious experience (1).
- Muslims believe that they can gain a personal understanding of Allah through religious experiences (1).

Other valid answers will be accepted.

2 One mark will be awarded for providing each reason and a second mark for development of the reason up to a maximum of four marks. (4)
- Religious experiences reveal the nature of Allah. Muslims believe that Allah's power is shown by revealing himself to prophets such as Muhammad (1). For example, visions and miracles show the power Allah has (1).
- Religious experiences strengthen faith in Allah (1), for example Muhammad's religious experiences confirm that Allah wants to connect with humanity (1).

- Prophet Muhammad received the Qur'an through a religious experience (1). This final perfect message from Allah began the religion of Islam (1).

Other valid answers will be accepted.

118 The design argument

1. One mark will be awarded for each point identified up to a maximum of three marks. (3)
   - The design argument shows that Allah is omnipotent (1).
   - The design argument shows that Allah is benevolent (1).
   - The design argument shows that Allah is omniscient (1).
   - The design argument shows that Allah is the designer of the universe (1).
   - The design argument shows that Allah is transcendent (1).

   Other valid answers will be accepted.

2. One mark will be awarded for providing each way and a second mark for development of the way up to a maximum of four marks. (4)
   - Muslims will argue for the design argument, suggesting that Allah is the only good explanation for the design perceived within the world (1). The Qur'an gives the examples of rain, wind and clouds as evidence of the design in the world attributed to Allah (Surah 2) (1).
   - Muslims may argue that evolution was part of Allah's design for the world (1). They believe scientific criticisms that try to damage the view that Allah designed the world can be used as part of the Islamic explanation to strengthen their argument (1).
   - Muslims may argue that bad design in the world does not disprove the design argument (1). Bad design may have a purpose that humans are not yet aware of (1).

   Other valid answers will be accepted.

119 The cosmological argument

1. One mark will be awarded for providing each characteristic and a second mark for development of the characteristic up to a maximum of four marks. (4)
   - The cosmological argument reveals that Allah is omnipotent (1). He is shown to have the power to create everything within the universe, including humans (1).
   - The cosmological argument reveals that Allah is benevolent (1). He cares for his creation and created everything humans needed, including food, water and shelter (1).
   - The cosmological argument reveals that Allah is omniscient (1). He was able to see what he created and did it in such a way that it all worked together (1).

   Other valid answers will be accepted.

2. One mark will be awarded for providing each reason and a second mark for development of the reason up to a maximum of four marks. (4)
   - Muslims believe the cosmological argument proves that there is a creator of the universe – Allah (1). Muslims accept that only Allah, who is omnipotent, could have created the universe (1).
   - Muslims believe that the cosmological argument reinforces teachings in the Qur'an (1). Surah 79:27 says, referring to the universe, 'Are you more difficult to create, or is the heaven that He constructed?' (1).
   - Muslims believe the cosmological argument proves that the universe has a creator who is benevolent towards his creation (1). Al-Ghazali put forward the 'kalam' version of the cosmological argument, which stated that there must be a cause of the universe (1).

   Other valid answers will be accepted.

120 The existence of suffering

1. One mark will be awarded for each point identified up to a maximum of three marks. (3)
   - The existence of suffering challenges whether Allah exists (1).
   - The existence of suffering questions whether Allah is omnipotent (1).
   - The existence of suffering questions whether Allah loves his creation (1).
   - The existence of suffering questions whether Allah is omniscient (1).
   - The existence of suffering questions whether Allah is just (1).

   Other valid answers will be accepted.

2. One mark will be awarded for providing each reason and a second mark for development of the reason up to a maximum of four marks. (4)
   - Suffering challenges the power of Allah (1). Muslims may question why Allah doesn't prevent the excessive amount of suffering that people face if he is able to do something about it (1).
   - Suffering calls into question whether Allah is all-loving (1). The Qur'an says 'In the Name of Allah, the Most Beneficent, the Most Merciful …' (Surah 1:1), which suggests his benevolence, but this is challenged by the presence of suffering in the world (1).
   - The existence of suffering calls into question whether Allah is omniscient (1). Muslims might question why Allah does nothing to help those who suffer if he knows everything that happens in the world (1).

   Other valid answers will be accepted.

121 Solutions to the problem of suffering

1. One mark will be awarded for providing each way and a second mark for development of the way up to a maximum of four marks. (4)
   - Muslims may respond by joining a charity that works to help those who are suffering (1). For example, they could volunteer for or make a donation to Muslim Aid, which responds to disasters (1).
   - Muslims may pray more often for those who are suffering (1). Muslims believe Allah will listen to their prayers and help those who are suffering by giving them the strength to cope (1).
   - Muslims could read the Qur'an and share its message about suffering with those who are affected (1). Teachings that tell Muslims to 'seek help through patience and prayer' (Surah 2:153) may encourage them not to give up (1).

   Other valid answers will be accepted.

2. One mark will be awarded for providing each teaching and a second mark for development of the teaching up to a maximum of four marks. One further mark will be awarded for any relevant source of wisdom and authority. (5)
   - The Qur'an teaches Muslims to turn to prayer to cope with suffering (1). Muslims believe they should put their faith in Allah and pray for the strength to cope with suffering (1): 'O you who have believed, seek help through patience and prayer. Indeed, Allah is with the patient.' (Surah 2:153) (1)
   - The Qur'an teaches Muslims that suffering is a test of their faith from Allah (1). They believe they should not question why they suffer, but instead accept that it has a higher purpose (1): 'And We will surely test you with something of fear and hunger and a loss of wealth and lives and fruits, but give glad tidings to the patient, Who, when disaster strikes them, say, "Indeed we belong to Allah, and indeed to Him we will return."' (Surah 2:155–156) (1)
   - Muslims believe they should use the presence of suffering in the world to develop positive characteristics like Allah by praying for strength (1). Muslims believe suffering helps them to appreciate the good in the world and makes them stronger (1): 'O you who have believed, seek help through patience and prayer. Indeed, Allah is with the patient.' (Surah 2:153) (1)

   Other valid answers will be accepted.

UNIT 8: EQUALITY

122 Human rights

1 "Muslims should always support human rights." Be sure to make your points specific, and refer to teachings and views, as you are instructed. You can support your arguments with Qur'anic or other teachings. Make sure you give balanced views and then draw a conclusion – make sure you say why this is your conclusion. (12)

Arguments for the statement:
- Many Muslims believe that standing up for the rights of others is a duty given to them by Allah. They believe that Allah created all humans to be equal, an idea that is reinforced in the Qur'an: 'And of His signs is the creation of the heavens and the earth, and the difference of your languages and colours' (Surah 30:22). This recognises that differences between people do not matter and all people are equal. Muslims believe that they should help to ensure equality is attained for all humans.
- There are examples of Muhammad standing up for the rights of others – particularly women and children. Muslims believe they should follow the example of Muhammad, as he was the prophet chosen by Allah to guide them.
- The Qur'an includes teachings that are seen to support human rights and to ensure justice is attained: 'O you who have believed, be persistently standing firm for Allah, witnesses in justice, and do not let the hatred of a people prevent you from being just' (Surah 5:8). Muslims believe that Allah is just and so they should also try to be just.

Arguments against the statement:
- Some Muslims may believe that although human rights are important, it may be acceptable to deny people certain rights in some circumstances. For example, if a person's freedom has been taken away from them as punishment for a crime, they should accept this.
- Some human rights – for example, same-sex marriage – may conflict with traditional Islamic beliefs. As some Muslims do not accept same-sex marriage due to Islamic teachings, they would not find it possible to stand up for these human rights.
- Muslims may believe that standing up for human rights is sometimes not the right action to take, for example in cases where they may come into conflict with the laws of the country in which they live. They may believe that only those in authority should get involved in such cases.

Other valid answers will be accepted.

123 Equality

1 One mark will be awarded for each point identified up to a maximum of three marks. (3)
- All Muslims pray at the same time (1).
- All Muslims complete the Five Pillars (1).
- All Muslims wear white on Hajj (1).
- All Muslims fast during Ramadan (1).
- All Muslims donate money in Zakah (1).

Other valid answers will be accepted.

2 One mark will be awarded for providing each reason and a second mark for development of the reason up to a maximum of four marks. (4)
- Islam teaches that humans were created equal by Allah and Muslims have a duty to work to achieve this (1). Muslims believe that they should stand up and help those who are not treated equally, such as those living in poverty (1).
- Muslims believe that as Allah is just they should also be just and work towards equal treatment of others (1). Muslims should 'be persistently standing firm in justice, witnesses for Allah' (Surah 4:135), suggesting that they should stand up for justice and equality for those who do not have it (1).
- Practices in Islam such as donating money in Zakah, which is a duty, demonstrate how all Muslims are expected to work towards equality (1). Sharing money through annual charitable donations helps to address financial inequality in the world (1).

Other valid answers will be accepted.

124 Religious freedom

1 "Religious freedom is important in a multifaith society." Be sure to make your points specific, and refer to teachings and views, as you are instructed. You can support your arguments with Qur'anic or other teachings. Make sure you give balanced views and then draw a conclusion – make sure you say why this is your conclusion. (12)

Arguments for the statement:
- Some Muslims believe that religious freedom is important because of the many benefits it brings to society. It allows different groups to interact and share their faiths, leading to greater understanding. It also gives Muslims the opportunity to connect with people from other faiths in interfaith networks in order to work towards greater justice and equality in society.
- Some Muslims believe that although Islam is the true faith and the final message from Allah, other faiths also contain important elements of truth that should be respected. Islam recognises many prophets from the religions of Christianity and Judaism, for example Abraham, Noah and Moses.
- Some Muslims believe that as long as a person is righteous, they will be favoured by Allah, regardless of their religion. This shows that all faiths are equally valid and Muslims accept that there are many ways to achieve their goal of paradise after death.

Arguments against the statement:
- Some Muslims do not accept religious freedom, as they believe that Islam is the only true faith and that Muslims have a duty to introduce Islam to non-Muslims. They believe other faiths do not convey the complete truth and that only Islam contains the final correct message from Allah.
- Some non-religious people may feel that complete religious freedom is wrong and that some faith practices should not be accepted in an increasingly atheist society. They may object to the practices of some religions, for example the way animals are killed for halal meat in Islam or the idea that Friday is a holy day.
- Some Muslims may believe that although it is an important goal, there is too much opposition to religious freedom and tolerance in today's society for it to be overcome. Muslims may feel that they increasingly face unfair discrimination or intolerance as a result of terrorist acts by minority extremist groups.

Other valid answers will be accepted.

125 Prejudice and discrimination

1 One mark will be awarded for providing each reason and a second mark for development of the reason up to a maximum of four marks. One further mark will be awarded for any relevant source of wisdom and authority. (5)
- Muslims believe that prejudice and discrimination go against teachings, such as those found in the Qur'an, that Allah created all people as equal but different (1): 'We have created you from male and female and made you peoples and tribes that you may know one another.' (Surah 49:13) (1)
- Muslims follow the teachings of Muhammad, who emphasised the importance of treating all people as equal in his final sermon (1): 'All mankind is descended from Adam and Eve' (Muhammad). This shows there is no difference between humans and that they should be treated equally (1).
- Muslims believe that it is important to be tolerant of other religions and to educate others about religion rather than discriminating against them if they are of a different faith (1). Many Muslims work as members of interfaith groups to challenge inequality in the world (1).

Other valid answers will be accepted.

126 Racial harmony
1. Award one mark for each point identified up to a maximum of three. (3)
   - All mankind is descended from Adam and Eve (1).
   - All humans are created equal by Allah (1).
   - All Muslims are equal in the ummah (1).
   - Muhammad taught that there is no difference between people from different races (1).
   - The Qur'an teaches that all races are equally valid (1).

   Other valid answers will be accepted.
2. One mark will be awarded for providing each reason and a second mark for development of the reason up to a maximum of four marks. (4)
   - Muslims believe that all humans from all races were created equal by Allah to live in peace together (1). This is reinforced in the Qur'an: 'We have created you from male and female and made you peoples and tribes that you may know one another.' (Surah 49:13) (1)
   - Muhammad taught about the importance of racial harmony in his last sermon (1): 'an Arab is not better than a non-Arab and a non-Arab is not better than an Arab' (Muhammad). This shows that all people are of equal value and should be treated the same (1).
   - Muslims are all part of the greater Islamic community – the ummah – and are all considered equal regardless of race (1). Islamic practices such as following the Five Pillars reflect this, as all Muslims perform the same actions wherever they happen to be (1).

   Other valid answers will be accepted.

127 Racial discrimination
1. One mark will be awarded for each point identified up to a maximum of three marks. (3)
   - Racial discrimination is wrong because Allah created all humans equal (1).
   - Muhammad taught that all humans are descended from Adam and Eve and are equal (1).
   - The Qur'an recognises both diversity and equal value among people (1).
   - Muhammad taught that there is no difference between people of different races (1).
   - Muslims of all races are considered equal in the ummah (1).

   Other valid answers will be accepted.
2. One mark will be awarded for providing each reason and a second mark for development of the reason up to a maximum of four marks. (4)
   - Muslims believe that all people are descended from Adam and Eve and so deserve to be treated the same (1). Racial discrimination can lead to races being attacked, which is wrong (1).
   - Muhammad taught in his last sermon that all races were equal (1). Racial discrimination can lead to races being targeted and misunderstood (1).
   - The Qur'an teaches that while there is diversity between people, all races are still equal (Surah 30:22) (1). This idea is reflected in the Muslim idea of the ummah, which promotes unity rather than difference as all Muslims perform the same acts regardless of race (1).

   Other valid answers will be accepted.

128 Social justice
1. One mark will be awarded for each point identified up to a maximum of three marks. (3)
   - The Qur'an teaches Muslims to help each other (1).
   - Muslims believe they will be judged after death on how they contributed to social justice (1).
   - Islam teaches that everyone is human and deserves human rights (1).
   - Shari'ah law promotes ideas of social justice (1).
   - The Five Pillars promote ideas of social justice (1).

   Other valid answers will be accepted.
2. One mark will be awarded for providing each reason and a second mark for development of the reason up to a maximum of four marks. (4)
   - Allah is considered to be just and Muslims believe they should also behave with justice towards others (1). Muslims believe that Allah will judge them after death on how they have behaved (1).
   - The Qur'an talks of the duty that Muslims have to work for social justice by helping others: 'So they who have believed in him, honoured him, supported him and followed the light which was sent down with him – it is those who will be the successful' (Surah 7:157) (1). Muslims believe that working for social justice will create more equality in the world (1).
   - Muslims must give Zakah every year, which is one of the Five Pillars (1). Zakah money is usually given to charities and is used to help the poor in society and to tackle issues of social injustice (1).

   Other valid answers will be accepted.

129 Wealth and poverty
1. "All Muslims should share their wealth with others." Be sure to make your points specific, and refer to teachings and views, as you are instructed. You can support your arguments with Qur'anic or other teachings. Make sure you give balanced views and then draw a conclusion – make sure you say why this is your conclusion. (12)

   Arguments for the statement:
   - Muslims are taught to share their wealth with others through charity. Zakah is one of the Five Pillars and it is a duty in Islam for Muslims to donate 2.5 per cent of their income annually. Muslims do this to support the poor and to reduce poverty, which is a key teaching in the Qur'an: '[true] righteousness is [in] one who … gives zakah.' (Surah 2:177)
   - Muslims are taught that wealth is a gift from Allah and should be used honestly to help others: 'be steadfast in prayer and regular in charity' (Surah 2:110). Many Muslims voluntarily support charities such as Islamic Relief or Muslim Aid.
   - Muslims believe that they will be judged after death on how they have acted towards others during their lives. Sharing their money with others is believed to please Allah and will help them to achieve their goal of paradise.

   Arguments against the statement:
   - Some Muslims may believe that although wealth is not ultimately the most important thing in life, it is a gift from Allah and therefore not a bad thing.
   - Some Muslims may believe that they can offer more practical help to others instead of giving money. They may think that volunteering with a charity can bring greater benefits to those in need.
   - Some Muslims may believe that it is not always possible to share wealth with others, such as in cases where people may not be able to afford to give Zakah.

   Other valid answers will be accepted.

130 (a) type questions
1. One mark will be awarded for each point identified up to a maximum of three marks. (3)
   - One of the Six Beliefs is Tawhid (1).
   - One of the Six Beliefs is a belief in angels (1).
   - One of the Six Beliefs is the authority of holy books (1).
   - One of the Six Beliefs is acceptance of the prophets (1).
   - One of the Six Beliefs is a belief in life after death (1).

   Other valid answers will be accepted.
2. One mark will be awarded for each point identified up to a maximum of three marks. (3)
   - The Qur'an was revealed to Muhammad (1).
   - The Qur'an was revealed over 23 years (1).
   - The Qur'an came directly from Allah (1).
   - The Qur'an helps guide Muslims (1).

- The Qur'an tells Muslims how Allah wants them to live their lives (1).

Other valid answers will be accepted.

3 One mark will be awarded for each point identified up to a maximum of three marks. (3)
- Muslims will want to follow the laws of Allah (1).
- Muslims will try to live good lives in order to be rewarded in the afterlife (1).
- Muslims will constantly be aware of their thoughts, beliefs and actions (1).
- Muslims will try to help others as this is what Allah wants (1).
- Muslims will try to perform the Five Pillars for Allah (1).

Other valid answers will be accepted.

4 One mark will be awarded for each point identified up to a maximum of three marks. (3)
- Muslims believe that sex is an act of worship (1).
- Muslims believe that the purpose of sex is procreation (1).
- Muslims believe that sex fulfils physical, emotional and spiritual needs (1).
- Muslims believe that sex should only take place within marriage (1).
- Adultery is forbidden in Islam (1).

Other valid answers will be accepted.

5 One mark will be awarded for each point identified up to a maximum of three marks. (3)
- Divorce is allowed in Islam as a last resort (1).
- Divorce is hated by Allah (1).
- The Qur'an contains guidelines on divorce (1).
- A couple are expected to try to reconcile before considering divorce (1).
- A Muslim man can divorce a woman (1).

Other valid answers will be accepted.

6 One mark will be awarded for each point identified up to a maximum of three marks. (3)
- The Shahadah is recited in public (1).
- The Shahadah is spoken before death (1).
- The Shahadah is whispered into the ears of newborn babies (1).
- The Shahadah is part of the adhan (1).
- The Shahadah is recited daily by Muslims (1).

Other valid answers will be accepted.

7 One mark will be awarded for each point identified up to a maximum of three marks. (3)
- Khums is given by Shi'a Muslims (1).
- Khums is 20 per cent of extra income (1).
- The descendants of Muhammad receive khums (1).
- Khums can be used to build Islamic schools (1).
- Khums can be used to help the poor and needy (1).

Other valid answers will be accepted.

8 One mark will be awarded for each point identified up to a maximum of three marks. (3)
- During Id-ul Fitr homes will be decorated (1).
- During Id-ul Fitr special mosque services will be held (1).
- During Id-ul Fitr Id cards will be sent to friends and family (1).
- During Id-ul Fitr a celebratory meal will be shared (1).
- During Id-ul Fitr extra prayers will be said to thank Allah (1).

Other valid answers will be accepted.

9 One mark will be awarded for each point identified up to a maximum of three marks. (3)
- Muslims believe that human life was created by Allah (1).
- The Qur'an says it is wrong to take away life (1).
- Muslims believe that human life is a gift from Allah (1).
- Muslims believe that humans have a soul (1).
- Islam teaches that only Allah can give and take away life (1).

Other valid answers will be accepted.

10 One mark will be awarded for each point identified up to a maximum of three marks. (3)
- Muslims can care for animals (1).
- Muslims can recycle items (1).
- Muslims can try to reduce pollution (1).
- Muslims can plant trees (1).
- Muslims can campaign to care for Allah's creation (1).

Other valid answers will be accepted.

11 One mark will be awarded for each point identified up to a maximum of three marks. (3)
- Justice is a key idea promoted in the Qur'an (1).
- Shari'ah law has strict rules on justice (1).
- The Five Pillars demonstrate ideas of justice (1).
- Muslims believe that Allah is just (1).
- Islam teaches that Muslims should stand up for justice (1).

Other valid answers will be accepted.

12 One mark will be awarded for each point identified up to a maximum of three marks. (3)
- Islam teaches that punishment can be a form of justice (1).
- Islam teaches that punishment can contribute to a peaceful society (1).
- Islam teaches that punishment allows criminals to change their behaviour (1).
- Islam teaches that punishment is needed to maintain law and order (1).
- Islam teaches that punishment helps to keep society safe (1).

Other valid answers will be accepted.

13 One mark will be awarded for each point identified up to a maximum of three marks. (3)
- Muslims can support Islamic Relief (1).
- Muslims can forgive those who do wrong to them (1).
- Muslims can campaign for people to work together (1).
- Muslims can work with different faiths for peace (1).
- Muslims can pray (1).

Other valid answers will be accepted.

14 One mark will be awarded for each point identified up to a maximum of three marks. (3)
- Visions help Muslims get closer to Allah (1).
- Visions show that Allah is omnipotent (1).
- Muhammad received visions (1).
- Visions are a way for Allah to communicate with humanity (1).
- Musa received a vision from Allah (1).

Other valid answers will be accepted.

15 One mark will be awarded for each point identified up to a maximum of three marks. (3)
- Muslims may pray (1).
- Muslims may donate money (1).
- Muslims may support Muslim Aid (1).
- Muslims may believe that suffering is part of a test in life (1).
- Muslims may read the Qur'an (1).

Other valid answers will be accepted.

16 One mark will be awarded for each point identified up to a maximum of three marks. (3)
- The Qur'an teaches that all mankind is descended from Adam and Eve (1).
- Islam demonstrates racial harmony through the ummah (1).
- Muhammad declared in his final sermon that there was no difference between Arabs and non-Arabs (1).
- The Qur'an teaches that no race is better than any other (1).
- Islam teaches that Allah created all humans to live together peacefully (1).

Other valid answers will be accepted.

131 (b) type questions

1 One mark will be awarded for providing each root and a second mark for development of the root up to a maximum of four marks. (4)
- One of the five roots of 'Usul ad-Din is Tawhid (1). Muslims believe in one God who is called Allah (1).

- One of the five roots of 'Usul ad-Din is Adl (1). This is divine justice as Allah is understood to be fair and just in his treatment of everything (1).
- One of the five roots of 'Usul ad-Din is Nubuwwah (1). This is prophethood and the belief that Allah appointed messengers to communicate with humanity (1).

Other valid answers will be accepted.

2 One mark will be awarded for providing each belief and a second mark for development of the belief up to a maximum of four marks. (4)
- Prophets are messengers from Allah (1). Muslims believe that Allah communicated with prophets such as Ibrahim in order to give important messages to humanity such as how to worship (1).
- Prophets are seen as role models for Muslims (1). For example, Ishma'il is praised for being patient and kind – characteristics that Muslims are expected to demonstrate (1).
- Prophets are believed to bring the words of Allah to humanity (1). Muhammad was given the Qur'an, which is the words of Allah (1).

Other valid answers will be accepted.

3 One mark will be awarded for describing each Muslim belief and a second mark for each contrasting Christian belief up to a maximum of four marks. (4)
- Islam teaches that individual sinners must ask for forgiveness before death in order to be forgiven (1). Christians believe that the sacrifice of Jesus atoned for the sins of the world (1).
- Islam accepts the idea of barzakh, which is the stage between death and a judgement from Allah (1). Christians accept the idea of purgatory, which is a waiting place following judgement where they go before their souls are cleansed in preparation for heaven (1).
- Muslims believe in angels who record the good and bad deeds of each individual Muslim (1). Christians do not believe that angels record the good and bad deeds of individual Christians (1).

Other valid answers will be accepted.

4 One mark will be awarded for providing each reason and a second mark for development of the reason up to a maximum of four marks. (4)
- Life after death is a key teaching in the Qur'an (1). Muslims believe Surah 17:71 talks of a Day of Judgement where Muslims will be judged (1).
- Muslims are taught that Allah will judge them after death (1). Muslims believe life is a test and that everything they do and think is recorded by angels for judgement in the afterlife (1).
- The Qur'an describes heaven and hell in detail (1). Heaven is a place of paradise and a reward, while hell is a place of torment and punishment (1).

Other valid answers will be accepted.

5 One mark will be awarded for providing each teaching and a second mark for development of the teaching up to a maximum of four marks. (4)
- Muslim parents are understood to have the responsibility of raising their children correctly (1). They are expected to introduce their children to the Islamic faith (1).
- The family is seen as the foundation of the ummah (1). It gives stability to society and is the basic unit of support for Muslims (1).
- The family is understood by Muslims to provide a loving and caring atmosphere in which to have children (1). Muslims believe they have a duty to marry and procreate in order to contribute to the religion of Islam (1).

Other valid answers will be accepted.

6 One mark will be awarded for providing each way and a second mark for development of the way up to a maximum of four marks. (4)
- The family can be supported through prayer (1). Muslim families attend the mosque together to show children how to worship Allah (1).
- Parents can attend classes to support and help them in their parental role (1). In these classes, help and advice can be given to support parents in raising their children correctly according to Islam (1).
- Families can celebrate important rites of passage together and within the Muslim community (1). Births, marriages and funerals help to bring people together and to celebrate the gifts Allah has given (1).

Other valid answers will be accepted.

7 One mark will be awarded for providing each teaching and a second mark for development of the teaching up to a maximum of four marks. (4)
- Gender prejudice and discrimination is wrong as Islam teaches that everyone is Allah's creation (1). Although men and women were not created to be the same, Muslims are taught that they were created to be of equal worth (1).
- Islam teaches that men and women will be judged in the same way after death (1). Men and women should not be treated differently as all are equal before Allah when they have to account for their actions on Earth (1).
- Men and women are understood to have the same rights in terms of Islam and pleasing Allah (1). Islam gives men and women equal responsibility to marry, have a family and care for Allah's creation (1).

Other valid answers will be accepted.

8 One mark will be awarded for providing each purpose and a second mark for development of the purpose up to a maximum of four marks. (4)
- The Ten Obligatory Acts are duties all Shi'a Muslims should perform (1). They help to guide Muslims in how they should live their lives (1).
- The Ten Obligatory Acts offer ways of getting closer to Allah (1). They are all actions – for example, prayer – which Allah expects Muslims to perform (1).
- The Ten Obligatory Acts help Muslims to achieve their goal of paradise in the afterlife (1). Islam teaches that through performing Sawm, giving Zakah and following the other acts Muslims will please Allah and be rewarded with heaven when they die (1).

Other valid answers will be accepted.

9 One mark will be awarded for providing each condition and a second mark for development of the condition up to a maximum of four marks. (4)
- One condition is that there has to be a just cause for lesser jihad (1). It should be fought to protect or defend Islam (1).
- One condition is that it should be fought as a last resort (1). All other ways of trying to resolve the conflict – for example, talking and working together – should have been tried first (1).
- One condition is that minimum amounts of suffering should be caused (1). Human life is sacred as it was created by Allah, so it should not be threatened through fighting unless absolutely necessary (1).

Other valid answers will be accepted.

10 One mark will be awarded for providing each belief and a second mark for development of the belief up to a maximum of four marks. (4)
- Muslims believe that all life was created by Allah (1). The Qur'an details how Allah created the world and everything in it, including humans (1).
- Muslims believe that Allah created balance in the universe (1). Examples include night and day or the sea and the land (1).
- Muslims believe that it took long periods of time to create the universe (1). Islam teaches in the Qur'an that Allah intended to create the universe and did it over a long period of time, one part at a time (1).

Other valid answers will be accepted.

11 One mark will be awarded for providing a teaching and a second mark for development of the teaching up to a maximum of four marks. (4)

- Islam teaches that all human life is sacred, so euthanasia is wrong (1). Muslims are taught that as Allah created human life, only he can take it away (1).
- Islam teaches that suffering has a purpose and that euthanasia is wrong (1). The Qur'an teaches that only Allah has the right to decide when a person's life should end (Surah 3:145) (1).
- Islam teaches that there are alternatives to euthanasia (1). Hospices allow people to die with dignity so they do not need to end their lives through euthanasia (1).

Other valid answers will be accepted.

12 One mark will be awarded for providing each teaching and a second mark for development of the teaching up to a maximum of four marks. (4)
- The Qur'an teaches that Allah is compassionate and merciful (Surah 64:14) (1). Muslims believe that they should also develop these characteristics and forgive those who do wrong to them (1).
- Muhammad taught that if a person is sorry they should be forgiven (1). Muslims believe that Islam is a religion of peace and that they should try to put this into practice by being forgiving when someone is sorry (1).
- Muslims are taught to be forgiving towards others in order to be rewarded in the afterlife (1). Islam teaches that, on the Day of Judgement, they will be judged by Allah on how they have behaved and that forgiving others will help them to achieve paradise (1).

Other valid answers will be accepted.

13 One mark will be awarded for providing each belief and a second mark for development of the belief up to a maximum of four marks. (4)
- The use of weapons of mass destruction (WMD) is wrong as innocent life will be threatened (1). Muslims believe that Allah created all life, thereby making it sacred, so that to threaten or take it is wrong (1).
- The use of WMD is wrong as damage will be done to the environment (1). Islam teaches that the universe is Allah's creation and a gift to humanity so it should be protected (1).
- The use of WMD is wrong as these weapons do not fit Islamic rules about war (1). Islamic Just War theory says that too much damage would be caused by WMD for them to be justified (1).

Other valid answers will be accepted.

14 One mark will be awarded for providing each way and a second mark for development of the way up to a maximum of four marks. (4)
- Muslims may argue that science and Islam both help to explain how the universe was created (1). Muslims can accept the 'Big Bang' theory alongside their views about Allah creating the world (1).
- Muslims believe that Allah does not need a cause that explains his existence, as critics of the cosmological argument argue (1). Allah is divine, as his characteristics show, and it is not possible for Muslims to fully understand him (1).
- Muslims may argue that there must be a first cause of the universe and this cause must be Allah (1). They believe the teachings of the Qur'an that contain words from Allah supporting the cosmological argument (1).

Other valid answers will be accepted.

15 One mark will be awarded for providing each way and a second mark for development of the way up to a maximum of four marks. (4)
- Muslims may support Islamic charities that try to help those facing inequality (1). Examples of Islamic charities include Muslim Aid and Islamic Relief (1).
- Muslims may pray for those facing inequality (1). They believe Allah listens to their prayers and will support them in bringing about change (1).
- Muslims in positions of authority may speak out against inequality in the world (1). There are examples of imams educating others about inequality and working for change (1).

Other valid answers will be accepted.

132 (c) type questions

1 One mark will be awarded for providing each characteristic and a second mark for development of the characteristic up to a maximum of four marks. One further mark will be awarded for any relevant source of wisdom and authority. (5)
- One characteristic shown in the Qur'an is Allah's omnipotence (1). His great power can be seen through his creation of the universe (1): 'Blessed is He in whose hands is dominion, and He is over all things competent – [He] who created death and life to test you [as to] which of you is best in deed – and He is the Exalted in Might, the Forgiving – [And] who created seven heavens in layers …' (Surah 67:1–3) (1)
- One characteristic shown in the Qur'an is Allah's immanence (1). Muslims believe that Allah is close to and involved in the world, as shown through his use of prophets to communicate with humanity (1): 'Say, [O believers], "We have believed in Allah and what has been revealed to us and what has been revealed to Abraham and Ishmael and Isaac and Jacob …"' (Surah 2:136) (1)
- Tawhid is shown in the Qur'an (1). Muslims accept that there is only one God (1): 'Say, "He is Allah, [who is] One."' (Surah 112:1) (1)

Other valid answers will be accepted.

2 One mark will be awarded for providing each teaching and a second mark for development of the teaching up to a maximum of four marks. One further mark will be awarded for any relevant source of wisdom and authority. (5)
- Muslims are expected to marry (1). Islam teaches that the purpose of marriage is to bring a man and woman together to have children (1): 'Marry those among you who are single.' (Surah 24:32) (1)
- Marriage is intended to be for life (1). The nikkah – the contract made in marriage – is not intended to be broken and divorce is strongly disliked (1): 'The most hated of permissible things to Allah is divorce.' (Hadith) (1)
- Muslims believe that they will be rewarded for being married (1). Islam teaches that Muslim couples who marry and have children are contributing to the ummah and to Islam (1): 'When a husband and wife share intimacy, it is rewarded.' (Hadith) (1)

Other valid answers will be accepted.

3 One mark will be awarded for providing each way and a second mark for development of the way up to a maximum of four marks. One further mark will be awarded for any relevant source of wisdom and authority. (5)
- Some Muslims think that men and women have different and unequal roles (1). Men, as the protectors and providers, are understood to be in charge of women (1): 'Men are in charge of women by [right of] what Allah has given one over the other.' (Surah 4:34) (1)
- Some Muslims think that men and women have different but equal roles (1). Men and women's roles complement each other, with men providing for their family while women look after and care for the family (1): 'O Mankind! Be dutiful to your Lord, Who created you from a single person.' (Surah 4:1) (1)
- Some Muslims may see women as having the more important role in the Islamic family (1). Women raise the family and take care of the home, including the husband's property if he is absent (1): 'The righteous among the women of Quraish are those who are kind to their young ones and who look after their husband's property.' (Sahih al-Bukhari 64:278) (1)

Other valid answers will be accepted.

4 One mark will be awarded for providing each reason and a second mark for development of the reason up to a maximum

of four marks. One further mark will be awarded for any relevant source of wisdom and authority. (5)
- Hajj is one of the Five Pillars of Islam (1). Muslims are expected to try to complete Hajj as it is a duty from Allah (1): 'The believing men and believing women are allies of one another. They enjoin what is right and forbid what is wrong and establish prayer and give zakah and obey Allah.' (Surah 9:71) (1)
- Hajj is seen to demonstrate equality between all Muslims (1). Muslims wear the same white clothing (ihram) and perform the same actions – for example, tawaf – to show that they are all the same (1): 'All people are equal like the teeth of a comb.' (Hadith) (1)
- Hajj demonstrates that all Muslims are part of the ummah (1.) This is the brotherhood of Muslims throughout the world and all are expected to complete Hajj (1): 'And proclaim to the people the Hajj.' (Surah 22:27) (1)

Other valid answers will be accepted.

5 One mark will be awarded for providing each response and a second mark for development of the response up to a maximum of four marks. One further mark will be awarded for any relevant source of wisdom and authority. (5)
- Some Muslims believe that other living things exist for the benefit of humans and so animals can be used for medical research (1). If it saves human life, experimentation is considered acceptable as human life was created by Allah to be special and to have dominion over the world (1): 'There is none amongst the Muslims who plants a tree or sows seeds, and then a bird, or a person or an animal eats from it, but is regarded as a charitable gift for him.' (Sahih al-Bukhari 3:513)
- Some Muslims may disagree with all animal experimentation arguing that animals are also Allah's creation and should therefore be respected (1). Muslims believe they have a duty of stewardship to care for animals and so they should not be used in experiments (1): 'Allah has appointed you his stewards over it.' (Hadith Bukhari) (1)
- Some Muslims may reject all animal experimentation because they believe they will be judged after death on how they have treated the world (1). As animals are Allah's creation, they have a right to be protected and not experimented on (1): 'And the earth He laid [out] for the creatures.' (Surah 55:10) (1)

Other valid answers will be accepted.

6 One mark will be awarded for providing each teaching and a second mark for development of the teaching up to a maximum of four marks. One further mark will be awarded for any relevant source of wisdom and authority. (5)
- Muslims believe that they should treat criminals fairly (1). The Qur'an teaches that prisoners should still be given human rights such as food, water and medical care (1): 'And they give food in spite of love for it to the needy, the orphan and the captive …' (Surah 76:8) (1)
- Muslims believe that criminals should have the right to a fair and just trial (1). Islam teaches that all people are created by Allah and therefore deserve fair treatment, including justice through fair punishment for criminals (1): 'O you who have believed, be persistently standing firm in justice …' (Surah 4:135) (1)
- Islam teaches that prisoners should not be tortured (1). Islam teaches that all humans are created by Allah and deserve respect as all life is sacred (1): 'O Mankind! Be dutiful to your Lord, Who created you from a single person.' (Surah 4:1) (1)

Other valid answers will be accepted.

7 One mark will be awarded for providing each teaching and a second mark for development of the teaching up to a maximum of four marks. One further mark will be awarded for any relevant source of wisdom and authority. (5)
- Islam teaches that war is allowed in certain circumstances (1). Islam teaches that it is acceptable to fight in order to defend the religion of Islam (1): 'And what is [the matter] with you that you fight not in the cause of Allah.' (Surah 4:75) (1)
- Muslims believe peace is important and that Muslims should work for peace, not war, in the world (1). As Allah is merciful and peaceful, all methods of peacefully resolving conflict should be tried before turning to war (1): 'And the servants of the Most Merciful are those who walk upon the earth easily, and when the ignorant address them [harshly] they say [words of] peace.' (Surah 25:63) (1)
- Muslims believe Allah is merciful and forgiving and that they should follow his example in times of conflict (1). Islam teaches that Muslims should avoid conflict and fight only in certain circumstances, such as to protect the innocent from harm or in self-defence (1): 'Fight in the way of Allah those who fight you.' (Surah 2:190) (1)

Other valid answers will be accepted.

8 One mark will be awarded for providing each way and a second mark for development of the way up to a maximum of four marks. One further mark will be awarded for any relevant source of wisdom and authority. (5)
- All Muslims attach some importance to religious experience as Muhammad himself underwent a religious experience (1) when the Qur'an was revealed to him (1): 'It is not but a revelation revealed. Taught to him by one intense in strength.' (Surah 53:4–5) (1)
- Some Muslims believe other forms of revelation are more important than religious experience (1). For example, some Muslims place greater importance on the Qur'an and the prophets as sources of authority than on religious experience (1): 'We have believed in Allah and what has been revealed to us and what has been revealed to Abraham and Ishmael and Isaac and Jacob …' (Surah 2:136) (1)
- Some Muslims, such as Sufis, are more mystical and place great importance on religious experience (1). They may even try to induce experiences as they feel these allow a personal connection to Allah (1): 'Those who do not know say, "Why does Allah not speak to us or there come to us a sign?"' (Surah 2:118) (1)

Other valid answers will be accepted.

9 One mark will be awarded for providing each teaching and a second mark for development of the teaching up to a maximum of four marks. One further mark will be awarded for any relevant source of wisdom and authority. (5)
- Religious freedom is important because it is a human right (1). Some Muslims believe that all religions should be respected because Islam recognises the truths of other faiths such as Christianity and Judaism (1): 'And Allah is hearing and knowing. Allah is the ally of those who believe.' (Surah 2:256–257) (1)
- Some Muslims may recognise that while all religions contain parts of the truth, only Islam contains the whole truth (1). They may believe that other faiths became corrupted and that Islam is the only way to understand Allah better (1): 'Say, "O People of the Scripture, come to a word that is equitable between us and you." But if they turn away, then say, "Bear witness that we are Muslims [submitting to Him]."' (Surah 3:64) (1)
- Some Muslims believe that it does not matter which religion a person belongs to (1). They accept that all righteous people will be favoured by Allah and therefore respect all religions (1): 'So whoever disbelieves in Taghut and believes in Allah has grasped the most trustworthy handhold with no break in it. And Allah is Hearing and Knowing.' (Surah 2:256) (1)

Other valid answers will be accepted.

133 (d) type questions

1 "All Muslims should get married." Be sure to make your points specific, and refer to teachings and views, as you are instructed. You can support your arguments with Qur'an or other teachings. Make sure you give balanced views and

then draw a conclusion – make sure you say why this is your conclusion. (12)

Arguments for the statement:
- Islam teaches that all Muslims should get married as this is what Allah intended. The Qur'an teaches: 'Marry those among you who are single' (Surah 24:32). Marriage was given by Allah as a gift for a man and woman in which they can join together and have children.
- Marriage is important to Muslims as it is believed to bring stability to society. Muslims believe the family unit, in which the couple are married, provides the ideal environment for raising good Muslim children within the Islamic faith.
- Islamic teachings do not support ideas of cohabitation as they hold traditional views about marriage. They believe that sexual relationships prior to marriage are wrong and Muslims often enter into arranged marriages to ensure a good match.

Arguments against the statement:
- Non-religious people may believe that marriage is no longer necessary in today's society. They accept that couples may wish to cohabit in order to get to know each other prior to considering marriage.
- Non-religious people may hold different views to Muslims about the purpose of marriage, believing that some couples may not wish to have children and therefore may not want to get married.
- Some Muslims may not want to get married. They may instead choose to dedicate their lives to Allah in another way.

Other valid answers will be accepted.

2. "Greater jihad is more important than lesser jihad." Be sure to make your points specific, and refer to teachings and views, as you are instructed. You can support your arguments with Qur'anic or other teachings. Make sure you give balanced views and then draw a conclusion – make sure you say why this is your conclusion. In this question, three of the marks awarded will be for your spelling, punctuation and grammar, and your use of specialist terminology. (15)

Arguments for the statement:
- Many Muslims will agree with the statement as greater jihad is emphasised more in the Qur'an, thus making it more important. This view is supported by Muhammad, who said: 'The person who struggles so that Allah's word is supreme is the one serving Allah's cause.'
- Greater jihad is an inner struggle in which Muslims strive to resist temptation and evil. Muslims would argue that overcoming temptation and evil on a daily basis and staying focused on the duties a Muslim has to perform is far harder than lesser jihad, therefore making it more important.
- Many Muslims understand greater jihad to be the true meaning of jihad itself, so giving it more importance. Greater jihad is a personal battle rather than a religious battle.

Arguments against the statement:
- Some Muslims may disagree with the statement, as lesser jihad is important when the religion of Islam as a whole is attacked. They may feel that defending Islam against global attack is more important than any personal battle.
- There may be times when lesser jihad becomes more important than greater jihad, so the statement may only be relevant at certain times. For example, if the religion of Islam is attacked, this becomes the most important thing.
- Because there are set criteria that must be followed, some Muslims may argue that lesser jihad is more important. Lesser jihad can only be declared by the right authority, if it is the last resort and for the purpose of defending Islam.

Other valid answers will be accepted.

3. "It is never right to fight." Be sure to make your points specific, and refer to teachings and views, as you are instructed. You can support your arguments with Qur'anic or other teachings. Make sure you give balanced views and then draw a conclusion – make sure you say why this is your conclusion. (12)

Arguments for the statement:
- Islam is a religion of peace, so this should always be the focus. There are many examples of how important peace is in Islam, including the way that Muslims greet each other with signs of peace. This shows that Muslims' first thoughts are always for peace and not conflict.
- Islam teaches that Allah created the world with the intention that peace would be part of his creation. Muslims place more emphasis on greater jihad – the personal daily struggle – than on lesser jihad – war.
- Muslims believe that the ummah demonstrates ideas of peace and that when there is conflict, the Muslim community should find peaceful methods to resolve it. The Qur'an advocates pacifism or passive resistance and does not support fighting (Surah 5:28).

Arguments against the statement:
- Some Muslims believe that war is sometimes necessary in order to bring about peace and that, therefore, fighting is justified in certain circumstances. One reason that they would accept is to defend the religion of Islam from attack.
- Some Muslims follow teachings in the Qur'an that support fighting. Islam is not a pacifist religion and some passages suggest that it is acceptable to fight and kill an enemy when necessary (Surah 9:5).
- Non-religious people may believe that fighting threatens life and is never right. They may feel that life is too valuable to be put at risk and that only peaceful methods should be used to resolve conflict.

Other valid answers will be accepted.

4. "It is wrong for Muslims to be wealthy." Be sure to make your points specific, and refer to teachings and views, as you are instructed. You can support your arguments with Qur'anic or other teachings. Make sure you give balanced views and then draw a conclusion – make sure you say why this is your conclusion. (12)

Arguments for the statement:
- Islam has many teachings on how Muslims should work to help others and act against social injustice. The Qur'an teaches that Muslims should be 'regular in charity' (Surah 2:110), and Muslims believe it is important to follow these teachings and to use their wealth for good purposes.
- Many Muslims would agree that Islam teaches the idea of sharing and caring for the poor. One of the Five Pillars of Islam is Zakah, which encourages Muslims to share their wealth with those in need.
- Muslims believe that it is important to be good khalifahs or stewards. They believe everything in the universe was created by Allah – including humans – and that they have a responsibility to use their money to help bring about greater equality.

Arguments against the statement:
- Some Muslims believe that wealth is a gift from Allah. Although it is not wrong for a Muslim to be wealthy, many Muslims often choose to give sadaqah – voluntary charitable donations – to use their money to help others where possible.
- Islam teaches that the more a person has, the more good they can do. Muslims believe they will be judged by Allah after death on the way they behaved and acted, which also includes whether they used their money wisely.
- Muslims understand that although it is not wrong for a Muslim to be wealthy, money is not the most important thing in life and it is more important to strive to live their lives as Allah intended.

Other valid answers will be accepted.

Notes

Notes

Notes

Notes

Published by Pearson Education Limited, 80 Strand, London, WC2R 0RL.

www.pearsonschoolsandfecolleges.co.uk

Copies of official specifications for all Pearson qualifications may be found on the website: qualifications.pearson.com

Text and illustrations © Pearson Education Ltd 2018
Typeset and illustrated by Kamae Design
Produced by Out of House Publishing
Cover illustration by Miriam Sturdee

The right of Tanya Hill to be identified as the author of this work has been asserted by her in accordance with the Copyright, Designs and Patents Act 1988.

First published 2018

British Library Cataloguing in Publication Data

A catalogue record for this book is available from the British Library

ISBN 978 1 292 13385 0

Copyright notice
All rights reserved. No part of this publication may be reproduced in any form or by any means (including photocopying or storing it in any medium by electronic means and whether or not transiently or incidentally to some other use of this publication) without the written permission of the copyright owner, except in accordance with the provisions of the Copyright, Designs and Patents Act 1988 or under the terms of a licence issued by the Copyright Licensing Agency, Barnard's Inn, 86 Fetter Lane, London EC4A 1EN (www.cla.co.uk). Applications for the copyright owner's written permission should be addressed to the publisher.

Acknowledgements
Pearson acknowledges the use of an extract from the following:
Lovelace, Ann and White, Joy, *Beliefs, Values and Traditions*, 2nd Edition, p102 © Heinemann (2002)

Notes from the publisher
1. While the publishers have made every attempt to ensure that advice on the qualification and its assessment is accurate, the official specification and associated assessment guidance materials are the only authoritative source of information and should always be referred to for definitive guidance.

Pearson examiners have not contributed to any sections in this resource relevant to examination papers for which they have responsibility.

2. Pearson has robust editorial processes, including answer and fact checks, to ensure the accuracy of the content in this publication, and every effort is made to ensure this publication is free of errors. We are, however, only human, and occasionally errors do occur. Pearson is not liable for any misunderstandings that arise as a result of errors in this publication, but it is our priority to ensure that the content is accurate. If you spot an error, please do contact us at resourcescorrections@pearson.com so we can make sure it is corrected.